A GUIDE TO
MANAGEMENT DEVELOPMENT TECHNIQUES

WHAT TO USE WHEN

KENNETH FEE

**KOGAN
PAGE**

First published in 2001

Kogan Page Limited
120 Pentonville Road
London N1 9JN
UK

Stylus Publications Inc.
22883 Quicksilver Drive
Sterling VA 20166-2012
USA

© Kenneth Fee, 2001

British Library Cataloguing in Publication Data

A CIP record for this book is available from the British Library.

ISBN 0 7494 3620 4

Contents

List of case studies   v
List of figures and table   vii
About the author   ix
Foreword   xi
Acknowledgements   xiii

Introduction   1

Chapter 1   **Saying what we mean**   6
What we mean by management development 6;
Splitting hairs 6; Organizational development 7; In the
doghouse 7; Management training 8; Training versus
education 8; Management development 9; Training
versus development 10; The learner-centred
perspective 10; A working model 10; Techniques or
methods? 13; Developer or trainer? 14

Chapter 2   **How managers learn**   15
Learner-centred learning 16; Types of management
learning 18; Self-managed learning 18; Experiential
learning 19; Learning styles 20; Activists, reflectors,
theorists and pragmatists 21; Determining an
intervention 22

Contents

Chapter 3 **Preparing for management development** **24**
A strategic framework 24; Career development 25;
Competence 26; Choosing providers 27; Choosing
techniques 28; Evaluation 29

———————————— **THE TECHNIQUES** ————————————

Chapter 4 **Courses and the classroom** **31**
Coursework 31 (The classroom 32; How long is a
course? 32; Sandwiches and blocks 37; Theory and
practice 38; Courses, not programmes 39; One to
one 39; Teaching/learning methods on courses 39)

Chapter 5 **Other off-the-job techniques** **55**
External events and visits 57; Games 61; Videos 66;
Psychometrics 69; Outdoor development 73; Open,
flexible and distance learning 77; E-learning 88;
Resource-based learning 95; Assessment techniques
103; Development centres 107

Chapter 6 **On-the-job techniques** **111**
Sitting by Nellie 113; Instruction 117; Secondment
121; Coaching and related techniques 126; Team
building 135; Action learning 139; Work-based
projects 143; Performance and development
review 147; Forms of learning record 153;
Discovery learning 159

Chapter 7 **Looking forward** **163**
Taking stock 163; The future of management
development 165

Appendix 1 **A-Z of management development techniques** **167**
Appendix 2 **Techniques and learning styles matrix** **169**
Index **173**

Case studies

1. **Bass Brewers**   33
   A traditional long course – a Diploma in Management Studies.
2. **The Department for International Development**   35
   How this organization implemented a programme of short
   courses.
3. **Michael Redfern**   52
   The use of innovation and creativity in coursework techniques.
4. **The American Society for Training and Development**   59
   A major international conference and exhibition.
5. **The Corporate Compendium**   63
   How British Telecom used a set of business simulation games.
6. **Video Arts' *Managing Problem People***   67
   An example of a videotape-based training package.
7. **Baker Hughes**   70
   Using the Myers-Briggs Type Indicator for management
   development.
8. **Oki**   75
   An outdoor development programme for team leaders.
9. **Standard Chartered Bank**   81
   A global distance learning programme.
10. **Motorola University**   85
    A corporate university.
11. **The growth curve of a new technique**   92
    The emergence of management development by e-learning.

12. **Standard Life**   **98**
A learning resource centre.
13. **Ashridge VLRC**   **100**
A virtual learning resource centre.
14. **The Scottish Qualifications Authority**   **104**
An awarding body's system of assessment for qualifications.
15. **Otis**   **108**
A development centre for a senior management team.
16. **Network Ireland**   **115**
How this organization promotes women in business through
shadowing, role modelling and other initiatives.
17. **Krib Naidoo**   **118**
A manager's experience of on-the-job instruction.
18. **Bob Gunning**   **123**
A manager's experience of secondment within the Royal
Bank of Scotland.
19. **Consignia**   **127**
A company-wide coaching programme.
20. **Colin George**   **131**
How this consultant implements executive coaching.
21. **Railtrack**   **136**
A team-building initiative across several companies in the
UK's railways.
22. **Huntsman Corporation**   **140**
An action learning programme for all managers and staff of
a petrochemicals plant.
23. **Bank of Scotland**   **144**
A programme of cross-functional, work-based projects.
24. **Scottish Power**   **149**
Performance and development review.
25. **Philips**   **151**
360-degree feedback in a career development programme.
26. **The MCI NVQ portfolio**   **156**
An example of a learning record – a portfolio of evidence of
competence.
27. **Kate Roberts**   **160**
On the developmental challenge of becoming a trainer.

Figures and Table

FIGURES

Figure 1.1 The semantics of education, development and training   11
Figure 1.2 The semantics of learning, education, development   13
            and training
Figure 2.1 Mumford's taxonomy of learning opportunities   17
Figure 2.2 Kolb's experiential learning cycle   20
Figure 7.1 Matrix of individual, group-work, off-the-job and   164
            on-the-job techniques

TABLE

Table A2.1 Techniques and learning styles matrix   170

About the author

Kenneth Fee lives in Glasgow and works mainly in Scotland, in the field of management and organization development. He is particularly interested in the imaginative applications of knowledge management, and in the interactive dimensions of e-learning. He has 20 years' management experience, holds an MA and an MBA, and is a Fellow of the Chartered Institute of Personnel and Development. This is his first book.

Kenneth Fee may be contacted by e-mail at:
kennethfee@hotmail.com

Foreword

Management development (MD) has been a subject of research and debate in the UK for over 50 years. However, questions concerning its meaning and purpose have yet to be resolved. This situation has arisen due to the preoccupations of both academics and professional practitioners, who are often too willing to engage in debate and dispute.

Most, though, would agree with a simple proposition: that a lack of agreement leads to unhelpful consequences. MD professionals, whether academics or organization-based professionals, are faced with a bewildering range of techniques and methods when designing MD programmes. Also, little guidance is available or provided to inform the selection of different techniques to achieve different purposes – at least not in one single volume. Kenneth Fee has produced in this book that much-needed guidance.

I should, at this point, declare an interest. I supervised Kenneth's MBA dissertation. This might be reason enough to agree to write this foreword. However, I am pleased to do so for the very simple reason that I can and do commend this book as a very useful addition to the literature on MD. It is not, nor does it claim to be, an academic examination of the subject. But it *does* claim to provide a practical guide to MD techniques – a claim that is met in a very successful fashion.

The inclusion of over 25 case studies and overviews of current debates helps to achieve this success. So, too, do the lists of further reading, which include some very useful Web addresses. The main success, though, lies in the book's essential content: the concise and clear descriptions and evaluations of the techniques themselves. Kenneth Fee's coverage is comprehensive and the orga-*nizing framework is sound and effective. A Guide to Management Development Techniques* is a book that I will certainly use to inform my own practice. I hope many others do the same.

Jim Stewart
Professor of Human Resource Development
Nottingham Business School

Acknowledgements

The author would like to thank the following for their comments and advice, and particularly for providing information for the case studies:

Graeme Ballantyne, Susan Broatch, Chris Brookes, Tom Brown, Graham Cater, Peter Chevis, Roy Davis, James Elson, Andrew Ettinger, Peter Farr, Colin George, Bob Gunning, Emmet Hedigan, Paula Hindes, Tony Horsfield, Alex Houston, Andy McAlpine, Brian McAvoy, Tony McCluskey, Alec McPhedran, Audrey Mathie, Phil Maughan, Maureen Meeke, Steve Mostyn, Krib Naidoo, Sharon O'Connor, John Pettigrew, Karen Pole, Chris Prince, Mike Redfern, Kate Roberts, David Robertson, Dave Sherrit, Julia Stevenson, Jim Stewart, John Todd, Gerry Topsom, Andy Tucker and Donna Willoughby.

Thanks are also due to all those organizations that allowed their details to be used for the case studies, to Alan Mumford for the use of his learning opportunities taxonomy and related material in Chapter 2, to David Kolb for use of his experiential learning cycle in Chapter 2 and to the editorial staff at Kogan Page for their patience with this fledgling author.

All of the ideas and opinions expressed are the author's own, and any mistakes or omissions are his responsibility alone.

Introduction

HOW WE VIEW MANAGEMENT DEVELOPMENT

Management development is a neglected subject. Of the thousands of books on management theory and practice published each year, themselves intended – at least in part – as a contribution to management development, few are concerned with directly addressing this subject. Many, perhaps most, business thinkers see management development as a subset of employee development, itself a subset of human resource management, which in turn is often seen as a support function, peripheral to the core disciplines of business. As a consequence of this thinking, management development is rarely discussed as a central plank of business strategy.

And yet: business organizations are run by managers; these managers need to be developed to their maximum potential in order to make the best possible contribution to their businesses; therefore management development is a fundamental driver of success in business organizations. This syllogism conveys the implication that management development ought to be central to business strategy, but the experience of many people in many organizations does not bear this out. Either there is a flaw in this logic, or many organizations are missing a significant opportunity.

The last few years of the 20th century saw the emergence of concepts like lifelong learning, the learning organization, corporate universities and knowledge management. These ought to have provided the context for management development to flourish, and it may yet, but the discipline lacks a champion with a compelling message. In the 1960s, Philip Kotler made the case for marketing to become the central discipline of business, bringing it out from the shadow of the sales function. Management development is still waiting for its Kotler.

If we explore the limited literature available, we find that it concentrates on the content of management development initiatives, or approaches to the subject. There has been a lack of attention to specific techniques, and although there is a great variety of them, little attempt has been made to evaluate their comparative strengths and weaknesses. This book aims to fill this gap.

THE ROLE OF THE MANAGER

It seems sensible, at the outset of a book on management development, to make clear what we mean by 'management' and what exactly a manager is. However, it may be best to avoid too academic a definition. Rather like an elephant, a manager is hard to pin down with a precise description, but we all know one when we see one.

In the (rather obvious) military analogy, managers are the equivalent of the officer class, clearly distinguishable from the rank and file. And in sport, nobody has any difficulty in recognizing the distinct role of the coaches or managers from that of the players. Sometimes it is harder to see what a manager's distinctive role is within a business organization – what, in fact, is the manager's function. Yet managers are as critical to business success as are, in their respective contexts, officers and sports coaches.

Managers are often regarded as the most important of an organization's human resources. There may be some who would prefer to identify the operatives producing a company's products as the most significant employees, at least in a manufacturing setting. But it is hard to translate such an economic determinist model into a service environment or into the public sector. The key consideration must be who adds value, and managers have the greatest opportunity to do this in the way they marshal resources and in the way they make decisions that shift the strategic direction of a company.

It is no coincidence that most large organizations single out the best minds for managerial roles, and invest the greater part of their training and development budgets in improving their managers. In this sense managers are widely seen to represent the cadre of most valuable employees within an organization – its leadership and its administrative engine. This book concentrates on managers because they are the drivers of business organizations. Developing them is about making a difference with the people who make a difference.

Considerable effort is exercised in organizations, and massive resources committed, to identifying managerial talent, nurturing it and ensuring it fulfils its potential. Career development and succession planning are essential activities for any organization that is serious about sustaining success over the long term. This book elaborates and evaluates the techniques at the disposal of such organizations.

When you see the term 'manager' in these pages, it is probably safe to assume in parenthesis 'or prospective manager', except in those rare cases where the context makes it redundant. The phrase is generally avoided to escape clumsy sentence formulation, but is included for deliberate emphasis where something is particularly relevant to the aspiring manager. References to 'learning managers' should be read as managers who are learning rather than as managers of learning.

HOW TO USE THIS BOOK

This book has been written to address the needs of human resources, training and development and management development managers, teachers, lecturers and facilitators of business education programmes, management development consultants, trainers and training providers, or any manager with an interest in the subject. It seeks to delineate the techniques, methods or tools available when making management development provision.

Chapters 1, 2 and 3 provide some background to management development, including discussions of semantics, approaches to learning and learning styles, and factors to take account of when preparing to undertake management development. While this gives context to what follows, any reader who just wants to find out more about specific techniques may simply skip these chapters.

The core of the book lies in Chapters 4, 5 and 6, which list, describe and evaluate coursework, other off-the-job, and on-the-job management development techniques. A section of each chapter is dedicated to each main technique known to be in current use within leading companies and public sector organizations in the UK and beyond. The book may be read as a continuous narrative, giving an overview of the range of available management development techniques, or it may be dipped into for reference to any single aspect.

The techniques are dealt with in what may seem an arbitrary sequence (although it aims to follow a natural progression), within the three broad categories, and the sections covering the techniques all follow the same format. At the start of each section, the technique is named, all its known alternative names are cited and it is marked to indicate whether it is suitable for use with individual managers (or prospective managers), groups of managers, or both.

In the narrative, each technique is treated in the following way:

- It is defined and described in some detail.
- It is analysed and evaluated to measure its strengths and weaknesses, to consider its costs and to indicate which learning style preference(s) it suits.
- Information is provided, where it is available, about the origins and history of the technique.
- A case study is provided, typically to look at a specific application of the technique, or to show how a leading organization has made recent use of the technique or is combining it with other techniques.

- Wherever possible, further reading of relevant books is suggested, and relevant Web sites are indicated.

Please note that the citing of books and Web sites does not imply endorsement of these works, or suggest their superiority over other sources – they are merely intended as a representative sample of useful material.

WHAT THIS BOOK DOESN'T COVER

In addressing management development, this book avoids as irrelevant any controversy over distinguishing collective management development from individual manager development. Techniques that may be used only with individuals, only with groups, or with either, are so indicated. But broader organizational development initiatives, despite impacting on managerial development among other things, are considered beyond our scope.

Thus no treatment is offered of schemes like Investors in People, the Business Excellence Model or Balanced Scorecard, although they may be mentioned in passing, where relevant.

Furthermore, this book sticks rigidly to techniques as defined in Chapter 2, and avoids methods that might more accurately be termed *approaches*. These would include, for example, John Adair's celebrated Action-Centred Leadership, or Richard Bandler's increasingly popular Neuro-Linguistic Programming (or NLP), or Ralph Coverdale's eponymous programme. These, along with concepts like emotional intelligence and knowledge management, are excluded not because they are held to have no impact on managers – far from it – but precisely because they are concepts, or systems, or approaches, and not specific techniques, which are the focus of our attention.

1

Saying what we mean

WHAT WE MEAN BY MANAGEMENT DEVELOPMENT

Before we go any further, we need to clarify what we are talking about. This is necessary because the terms 'management *development*', 'management *training*' and, to a lesser extent, 'management *education*' are often used interchangeably. Writers and practitioners frequently seem to use 'training and development' in the same loose, tautological way that many people refer to 'aims and objectives', where either term – but just one – is sufficient to describe their meaning. Moreover, different people use each of these terms to mean different things. We need to distinguish the three concepts and demonstrate how they fit within the overall context of learning.

SPLITTING HAIRS

A common opinion is that this is all pedantry: that picking over the exact meanings of words or phrases is self-indulgent, futile, unproductive or just splitting hairs.

There is a kernel of truth in these arguments, in the sense that it can focus attention inward, but in a work like this it is essential for clarity of understanding that we have a working definition of management development and thus can distinguish it from the other concepts. Precise use of language in defining and distinguishing the things we are discussing enables us to offer more accurate prescriptions for the use of these same things.

ORGANIZATIONAL DEVELOPMENT

A fourth term that is often thrown into this sort of discussion, and often confused with the other terms, is 'organizational development'. This is a red herring, as it clearly refers to a broader corporate audience for development activities than just managers, who are the focus of our concern. Good management development initiatives will usually result in the organization developing, but so too will good employee development initiatives that don't involve managers at all.

Some people may prefer the term 'organizational development' to 'training and development' simply because they prefer the sense of purpose that it conveys, but most people would recognize it as something broader. Certainly, that it is broader than management development should not be up for question.

IN THE DOGHOUSE

Managers sometimes prefer the term 'management development' to 'management training', but a cynic might suggest this is only because it *sounds* better – broader, more complex and perhaps more important. Training has strong associations with induction, elementary instruction, apprenticeships and generally lower-level education than a manager might aspire to.

The corollary is that universities, and other high-level education providers, rarely refer to their work as 'training' – and even then, only with the aspirational prefix 'professional'.

In many settings, being a 'trainee' has pejorative connotations. Anita Roddick, founder of The Body Shop, has said that 'training is something they do to dogs'. More formal definitions of training, or management training, tend to reflect this value judgement.

MANAGEMENT TRAINING

In 1991 the UK's Manpower Services Commission (MSC) developed the following working definition: 'Training is a planned process to modify attitude, knowledge or skill behaviour through learning experience to achieve effective performance in an activity or range of activities. Its purpose, in the work situation, is to develop the abilities of the individual and to satisfy the current and future needs of the organization' (Wilson, 1999: 4).

The expression 'learning experience' was deliberately chosen from the standpoint that they wished to blur any preconceived distinction between education and training, and to emphasize their common ground. The MSC adopted this position in a deliberate attempt to elevate the status of training, by borrowing some of the prestige of education, and their definition owes more to this desire than to any urge for clarity.

TRAINING VERSUS EDUCATION

However, most contemporary writers and practitioners take the view that education and training are different and distinguishable. Management training is generally understood to be about developing highly specific and immediately useful skills, whereas management education is perceived as facilitating a broad range of abilities. Education processes are regarded as being more theory- or knowledge-based, whereas training is more likely to focus on practical skills and be concerned with applying and implementing techniques and processes.

It is easy to find those who will argue that management training is something that should be implemented when skills can't so easily be learnt at the workplace, clearly regarding all training as comprising exclusively off-the-job activities, mainly consisting of training courses. And contrarily there are others, probably the majority, who associate the term 'education' more with the off-the-job course, and 'training' more with learning by doing, on the job.

Notwithstanding training practitioners seeking a broader context for their work, the consensus is that education is the broader process, providing a general background to an individual's development, while training is much more specific and short-term goal-focused. Education is more theoretical, while training is more practical.

MANAGEMENT DEVELOPMENT

Among those who adhere most closely to this consensus, there is a further shared position regarding the superior nature of management development. This is that management development embraces the entire process by which managers learn, progress and improve their competence to perform managerial tasks. And this is assumed to include both management education and management training.

Some relegate management education to just a kind of management schooling, presuming the context of a formal place of teaching – a college or university, or possibly a private training centre – and a definite focus on learning away from the workplace. And this definition also assumes such 'education' to be overwhelmingly theoretical, even intellectual, with no bridge to practical application.

The corresponding narrow definition of management training is a kind of mirror image of education, heavily practical in emphasis, taking place mainly on the job, eschewing theory and concentrating on skills development.

To complete the trinity, management development is often considered to bring together both of these and anything else that serves to help the individual learn (within the organizational context) and that furthers the needs of the organization overall.

So, one view is that education and training, at least in a management context, are narrower concepts than management development.

TRAINING VERSUS DEVELOPMENT

Some managers are comfortable with distinguishing training from development, but ignore the complication of 'education'. A common position arising from this view is that management training is about acquiring the skills associated with a specific management job role, while management development is about career development and progression within the organization.

It is possible to extrapolate from this an alternative view that training and development are narrower concepts than education.

THE LEARNER-CENTRED PERSPECTIVE

A third view is that education and training are inputs, and that 'development', like 'learning', is what the learner experiences. This view characterizes learning and development as being more useful and appropriate terms than training or education, since they are about outputs – results or outcomes – rather than inputs.

This seems too narrow a definition of development, denying it an active role as a tool, or input.

Furthermore, development and learning may be more relevant terms from the learner's point of view, and that is something organizations need to take account of, but this work is concerned with offering theoretical and practical guidance to organizations seeking to implement management development. We are examining the issues from the input side, and so although we need to have regard for the output implications, we need to describe and evaluate development techniques as they may be delivered.

A WORKING MODEL

In constructing a model to guide us, we need to have regard for the variety of opinions expressed above. Common to all of these is that training is the most basic process described by the various terms, and that development, while encapsulating training, is a broader concept.

Some writers and practitioners regard education as broader than development; some take the contrary view. The latter seems tenable only if education is limited in some way, as it is in the institutionally focused definition discussed above. Remarkably, it is often educationalists themselves who seek to promote this narrow definition of education, but perhaps only when discussing something like management development, as it seems scarcely credible they would adopt this view of their profession overall.

Therefore, our position is summarized by reference to Figure 1.1.

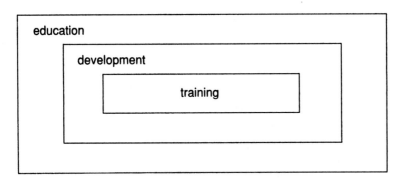

Figure 1.1   The semantics of education, development and training

In Figure 1.1, training is depicted as a subset of development. Training is the collective term for those learning activities that are usually operational and tactical in scope, and designed to address short-term or urgent needs. Development is the collective term for the broader range of learning activities that may be operational, tactical or strategic, for short- or longer-term purposes, more or less urgent and/or more or less important. Education is a still broader concept, encapsulating all development, including all training, but also incorporating other learning that defies classification as training or development.

Both training and development are highly specific concepts, with easily defined – often behavioural – objectives, whereas education is more wide-ranging. For example, it has been argued that university degrees in non-business or even non-vocational subjects, such as English literature or classics, provide a better grounding for a career in management than more specific training in business studies, including business degrees. The idea is that the academic discipline provides a better grounding for a variety of aspects of life, not just a management career. This only makes sense if we recognize a broader role for education.

Training and development are terms that address the range of learning measures that may be implemented by an organization with a view to achieving certain corporate goals. They encompass everything from the training of individuals to accomplish specific tasks, to organizational development initiatives. These exist within a wider world of education, which embraces not just the fulfilment of corporate objectives, but also learning that may accrue to the individual but not the organization, or to neither party. One practical example would be industry-wide education that happens to be of no direct benefit to a particular participating company; another would be vocational education for the individual that has no immediate relevance to his/her current employment.

So we have three levels of input: education, development and training.

The logical consequence of this model is that we identify education as the planned expression of a universe of learning. Thus training is a subset of development, which is a subset of education, in turn a subset of learning (see Figure 1.2). This model may be fallible, but it will support all of our descriptions and examples of management development.

Within the context of this model, management development is defined as the activities and processes, whether on the job or off the job, that facilitate cognitive and behavioural development, the acquisition of new skills, knowledge and understanding, and the development of competence.

Ideally, we should further refine this definition to stress behavioural change as the outcome of the learning process, and to emphasize the strategic dimension of development, especially to effect career progression and organizational development.

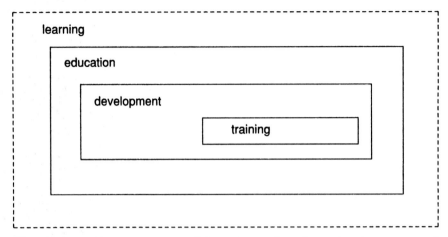

Figure 1.2 The semantics of learning, education, development and training

However, this would be at the expense of being succinct: accordingly, this is the working definition that we carry forward. 'Management development' is read as the core concept, of which 'management training' constitutes a small part, and which forms the bulk of 'management education', inclusive of that which is of direct benefit to business organizations.

TECHNIQUES OR METHODS?

This also seems an appropriate point at which to explain the choice of the term 'technique'. *The Concise Oxford Dictionary* defines a technique as a 'procedure that is effective in achieving an aim'. Most writers share a preference for this term, but some opt for the alternative term 'method'. The same dictionary defines a method as, among other things, a 'procedure for accomplishing or approaching something'. Thus these terms are taken to be synonyms in our context. The term 'management development techniques' is preferred in this book, but if the term 'management development methods' is occasionally deployed instead, no difference in meaning is intended.

DEVELOPER OR TRAINER?

In this book, the term 'trainer' is used to denote the individual, such as a lecturer, who is directly providing the management development. Despite our preference for development over training, somehow the alternative 'developer' just seems too contrived.

Further reading

Stewart, J (1999) *Employee Development Practice*, FT Pitman, London

Walton, J (1999) *Strategic Human Resource Development*, FT Prentice-Hall, Harlow

Wilson, J (ed) (1999) *Human Resource Development*, Kogan Page, London

Woodall, J and Winstanley, D (1998) *Management Development*, Blackwell, Oxford

2

How managers learn

Having been at pains to identify a distinctive role for managers, and to define management development as precisely as possible, the next point may seem perverse, but managers learn in just the same way as other employees, or indeed any other people. This truism may be valuable to those who are training very senior, potentially intimidating, managers for the first time.

As a general rule, managers are relatively intelligent, capable and often willing learners, and deserve to be treated as such. There should be no place in management development for techniques that demean the participants, nor for anything so simplistic that it insults their intelligence or wastes their time. The corollary of this is that managers can usually be counted on to respond to a challenge – they enjoy being stretched, and reward the trainer who is prepared to reach for exceptional outcomes.

The techniques explored in this book are very similar to those cited as *employee* development techniques, the main difference being that the latter would probably give far greater emphasis to techniques better suited to elementary training. Instead, this book deals in a more cursory way with such techniques – like sitting by Nellie, instruction, demonstration and discovery learning. There are beginners in management as in any other occupation, but those who achieve management positions have usually served time in other roles, sometimes quite senior ones, and have often undertaken considerable education and training in other disciplines. They may usually be presumed to be experienced learners.

Nevertheless, there are some general rules about how people learn that are particularly helpful in considering how managers learn. A full appreciation of how management development techniques work may be informed by an understanding of the learner's perspective, the characteristics of experiential learning, and models of individual learning styles. These matters have formed the substance of considerable academic attention in recent years, and the findings represent an established, if evolving, theory of learning.

LEARNER-CENTRED LEARNING

There is a long-held consensus among educationalists, training and development professionals, and commentators on human resource development (HRD), that all learning should be considered from the point of view of the learner: the phraseology of this philosophy is that learning should be 'learner-centred'. Alan Mumford typifies this school, may even be considered to be one of its leading exponents, so it is no surprise that his approach to management development commences from this position.

In his 1997 book, *Management Development: Strategies for action*, Mumford offers a simple taxonomy of 'learning opportunities' (see Figure 2.1). The problem with this is that it includes many opportunities that are difficult to plan, difficult, if not impossible, to measure, and many, not least one of Mumford's four categories in its entirety, go beyond the scope of what an employer can hope to control or even influence. This is not to dispute that these opportunities exist, or that they are all potential sources of development. But this is of little practical value to an organization looking to identify ways to improve its management, with a view to achieving new business goals.

Setting aside the obvious omissions from these listings, such as participating in courses or conferences, they do help give an overview.

Situations within the Organization	Process	People
	coaching	boss
meetings	counselling	mentor
task – familiar	listening	network contacts
– unfamiliar	modelling	peers
task force	problem solving	consultants
customer visit	observing	subordinates
visit to plant/office	questioning	
managing a change	reading	
social occasions	negotiating	
acquisitions, mergers	public speaking	
closing something down	reviewing, auditing	
	clarifying responsibilities	
Situations outside your Organization	walking the floor	
	visioning	
	strategic planning	
charity	problem diagnosis	
domestic life	decision making	
industry committee	selling	
professional meetings		
sports club		

Figure 2.1 Mumford's taxonomy of learning opportunities

Mumford's taxonomy presents a powerful case that any consideration of management development should take account not just of planned and deliberate development activities, but of informal learning, such as may arise from a variety of circumstances, often accidental, and from exposure to the practices of colleagues, especially senior colleagues. This is, consistently, a learner-centred approach. But what organizations need, in practical terms, is guidance and specific techniques to implement. Clearly, to be successful, each technique will need to be learner-centred, but that does not mean we cannot plan from the perspective of the implementer. Therefore we should discount the opportunities that Mumford himself acknowledges are 'fragmentary, insufficient, inefficient, only partially understood, and subject to the winds of circumstance'.

TYPES OF MANAGEMENT LEARNING

Mumford goes on to develop a model of management development, which classifies three types. These are:

1. *informal managerial* – accidental processes;
2. *integrated managerial* – opportunistic processes;
3. *formal management development* – planned processes.

The first two both lead to real and direct learning, but in the first type unconscious and insufficient, while in the second conscious and more substantial. In the third type, learning may not be 'real' as it may be in the detached, artificial climate of a course, but it is more likely to be conscious. Nevertheless, it is the third type that we focus on here, as these comprise the explicit techniques; the second type is of interest only insofar as the interventions may be planned, while the first type lies beyond the scope of planning.

When it comes to classifying the techniques, there is a broad consensus on the separation of techniques into on-the-job and off-the-job methods. We shall therefore deal with them in these categories, irrespective of how they fit within Mumford's typology or any other classification. The most commonly used off-the-job technique, the course, involves so many variations that it merits a chapter of its own. An alphabetical list of all of the techniques may be found in Appendix 1.

SELF-MANAGED LEARNING

A development from the theory of learner-centred learning is the notion that learning should be managed by the learners themselves. This starts from the assumption that there is a lot of under-exploited, latent knowledge within managers, and great learning potential arising from the synergy of bringing managers together and encouraging them to air their knowledge. A number of the techniques in this book, such as work-based projects and action learning, spring from this philosophy.

While this is true as far as it goes, if only self-managed learning techniques are used, managers are cut off from external stimulation and the introduction of new theories, ideas and experiences. Accordingly, some powerful techniques, like open learning, seek to combine elements of self-managed learning with theoretical input such as from traditional courses or resources.

Nevertheless, self-managed learning has been attracting a lot of interest lately, as the pendulum swings from more effective to more efficient techniques. Self-managed learning works best when there are adequate support mechanisms to substitute for the trainer or facilitator, such as the promotion of learning groups (eg action learning sets) and the use of learning contracts.

EXPERIENTIAL LEARNING

There is further common ground in the belief that managers learn best by experiencing things and then studying what they have experienced. This is not an anti-theoretical position, but a simple acknowledgement that management is a practical profession, in which theory must be applied to real situations and circumstances. The theory of experiential learning stresses the importance of managers experiencing things for themselves as the basis for their development. Techniques like discovery learning and sitting by Nellie implicitly follow this theory. The challenge for trainers using other techniques is to find ways to tease out, and draw upon, managers' experiences.

There is another way of looking at this. Experience may be the best teacher, but additional inputs help managers learn more effectively as well as more efficiently. In other words, experience is no substitute for planned management development. Peter Honey puts it very nicely on his Web site: 'learning from experience is tough, you get the test first and the lesson afterwards'.

So there is no contradiction in championing learner-centred learning, self-managed learning or experiential learning, and simultaneously taking a trainer-centred approach to describing techniques for supporting learning. Indeed, this is the very essence of the thinking of those who have given greatest consideration to individual learning styles.

LEARNING STYLES

The most widely recognized model informing our understanding of individual learning preferences is Kolb's learning cycle. David Kolb developed his model in 1984 (see Figure 2.2), although it was not until the 1990s, when Peter Honey and Alan Mumford adopted it as the foundation of their work on learning styles, that it became as well known as it is today.

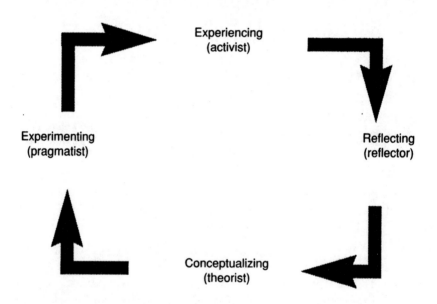

Figure 2.2   Kolb's experiential learning cycle

The idea is that the process of learning can be divided into four stages: acting, reflecting, conceptualizing and experimenting. Then, because learning is a continuous process, we return to the top of the cycle and go around again. However, there is another idea, reinforced by Honey and Mumford, which is that each learner – or, in our context, each manager – tends to have a preference for one of the four stages of the cycle. This is that manager's learning style preference.

The message behind the model is that trainers designing learning activities – and choosing development techniques – need to support each of the stages of the cycle. This not only ensures a complete learning experience, but also guarantees that every learner is able to use the style s/he prefers and therefore engage with the technique. The four stages of Kolb's cycle correspond to the four principal learning styles identified and promoted by Honey and Mumford.

ACTIVISTS, REFLECTORS, THEORISTS AND PRAGMATISTS

Thus the manager who prefers to concentrate upon acting – doing things and accumulating concrete experience – is characterized as an 'activist'. This type of learner emphasizes the top part of Kolb's cycle, 'experiencing'.

The manager who likes to spend time reviewing his/her experience and reflecting upon problems is characterized as a 'reflector', corresponding to the right-hand part of the cycle, 'reflecting'.

The manager who takes the most cerebral approach, the opposite of the activist, and focuses on understanding concepts, is a 'theorist'. This position corresponds to the bottom of the cycle, 'conceptualizing'.

And, lastly, the manager who likes to plan, explore options and test theories is a 'pragmatist', whose position corresponds with the left-hand part of the cycle, 'experimenting'.

Clearly it is too facile to categorize every manager as merely one of four rigid types: an activist, a reflector, a theorist or a pragmatist. None of us fits neatly into convenient pigeon-holes like this. But these are useful indicators of a predominant preference on the part of a manager, even if many individual examples are hybrids, and they are valuable reference points in constructing learning events.

In order to be effective, management development techniques need to accommodate the preferred learning styles of all four types. If they do not, then they risk failing the managers whose chosen styles are not included. Wherever possible, the examination of techniques in the following chapters will identify which techniques particularly suit which styles and, where this is the case, which techniques definitely exclude certain styles. This does not mean these techniques are unusable with that type of learner, but it does represent a significant constraint, which needs to be borne in mind when designing the learning experience. The best fit of management development techniques to preferred learning styles is summarized in a matrix in Appendix 2.

DETERMINING AN INTERVENTION

No technique will be successful if it is inadequately understood, poorly developed or clumsily implemented. Our consideration of each technique assumes diligence on the part of the trainer and that every effort has been made to make a success of it. We assume each technique is used in the most learner-centred way possible, takes account of experience even if the technique itself is not explicitly experiential, and takes full account of individuals' preferred learning styles.

And, clearly, there is a host of other factors affecting a manager's potential to learn in any given situation using any given technique. There is the manager's environment, including not just his/her physical surroundings but the organizational culture and climate, peer pressure, and time and space for learning. There is the manager's ability to learn, including experience of learning to learn, ease of transferring learning to work, his/her behaviour and acceptance of opportunities. And there is the manager's motivation to learn, including characteristics like enthusiasm, courage and resilience. These, along with preferred learning styles, should influence the management development professional's choice of techniques.

Further reading

Cunningham, I *et al* (ed) (2000) *Self Managed Learning in Action*, Gower, Aldershot

Honey, P and Mumford, A (1992) *Manual of Learning Styles*, Honey, Maidenhead

Kolb, D (1984) *Experiential Learning*, Prentice-Hall, New York

Mumford, A (1997) *Management Development: Strategies for action*, IPD, London

Pedler, M *et al* (1994) *A Manager's Guide to Self-Development*, McGraw-Hill, London

Web reference

www.peterhoney.com

3

Preparing for management development

A STRATEGIC FRAMEWORK

The classic approach to management development – and indeed all employee development – follows a simple cycle of identifying and analysing development needs, planning and designing a development intervention, implementing the intervention and evaluating its success. The last part of this process should lead into the identification of new and ongoing development needs, and so the cycle goes round.

On first impression, this may be viewed as a reactive system, merely responding to needs that arise or are reported and then working them through. However, the cycle may be driven proactively, by searching for needs and by constantly seeking ways to improve, even when no problems are being identified. Nevertheless, this remains an insufficient basis on which to conduct management development, if it is not linked to a strategic framework, a vision of where the organization needs to go, and what knowledge, skills and understanding its managers need to have now and will need to have in the future.

For individuals too, it is far too limiting to consider only what capabilities are lacking to fulfil current job functions. Each individual manager needs to follow a career path and prepare to be equipped for the challenges ahead, even when it is unclear what those challenges may be.

It may not be necessary to have an explicit management development plan, and indeed planning is now widely considered to be too inflexible an approach in a world of ever-increasing change. But just as an organization needs to have goals and a shared sense of how to achieve them, so management development needs a compass to steer by. For example, a sense of the future size of an organization's management population will drive its graduate recruitment efforts, and thence its graduate development programme. And the comparative costs of headhunting senior executives from competitors will inform the scale of investment in succession planning and development of managerial talent from within.

CAREER DEVELOPMENT

When we consider management development, we are looking at two distinct but related interests: the development of individual managers in pursuit of their career goals, and the development of a management cadre to staff an employing organization. These interests frequently coincide, but can sometimes conflict, and it is part of the role of the management development professional to do whatever is necessary to help them dovetail.

Managers are increasingly being encouraged to undertake continuous professional development (CPD) both by their industrial/professional bodies and by their employers. The career management outlook fostered by CPD is useful not just to individual managers but also to their employing organization, as it helps focus managers on skills and knowledge acquisition, and on fulfilling their potential.

Organizations are increasingly seeking to formalize and implement measures that help meet their strategic objectives: such initiatives include identifying high potential, nurturing talent and succession planning. For individual managers, these are opportunities both to move on in the organization and to acquire capabilities that may be useful later in their careers.

Career development planning is about taking a deliberate corporate approach to ensuring that managers' careers may be fulfilled within the organization, exposing them to opportunities that will both satisfy individual needs for personal growth and exploit these greater capabilities for the immediate benefit of the organization. Many management development techniques have been devised with these twin aims in mind. Among the techniques that specifically facilitate succession planning are development centres, and performance and development reviews. Another key area is the use of managerial competence development systems.

COMPETENCE

In recent years, management development professionals have devoted significant attention to the question of managerial competence. This has mirrored, at the individual level, growing interest in the distinctive competences of organizations. Some prefer the term 'competency', especially when considering individual competences as distinct from the general concept, but the single term 'competence' (along with its plural, 'competences') is used in this book.

Initially there was some resistance to the concept. Some commentators felt that competence implied a minimal standard, and that striving merely for competence limited the reach of managers. Instead, they counter-posed the pursuit of excellence, but this has proved to be a false opposition: competence is now widely regarded as a business imperative, representing no contradiction with the desirable goal of excellence.

Interest in managerial competence was first sparked in the United States in the 1970s by the American Management Association, and led to the recognition and acceptance of clusters of competences emphasizing personal effectiveness. These tended to be skills-based or behavioural competences, whereas the UK approach, which didn't follow until the late 1980s, used a model of functional competence. The UK system focuses on individual job functions, and emphasizes consistent measurement of work outcomes, expressed in the National Management Standards and National Vocational Qualifications (see Case Study 26).

Managers and trainers have a choice, therefore, between behavioural and functional competences, which need not be mutually exclusive, and a further choice between using generic competences, of which the UK National Management Standards are just one example, or devising their own, tailored to the circumstances of their own organization or industry. All of these choices share the same characteristics of being highly structured approaches and having a strong work-based focus. They are not universally applied, but in many organizations they are now well established and have become the norm for all recruitment, job design, performance management and development. Advocates of competences argue strongly that they provide an invaluable framework for managers to relate their development to their work.

The use of a competence-based approach is not of itself a management development technique, but many of the techniques in this book are readily adaptable to the approach and indeed some have been influenced by it. Where a technique is strongly linked to the issue of competence, special note is made within each relevant section.

CHOOSING PROVIDERS

For many management development professionals, a constant and critical question is whether to make management development provision internal or external, that is, whether to use the in-house resources of an organization, or instead to contract the services of an outside provider, like a business school or a firm of consultants.

It used to be the norm for large organizations to retain large teams of trainers on the staff. However, these have been persistently cut back over the last 20 to 30 years, as it became apparent that trainer skills could be bought in more cheaply, as and when required. Many aspects of management development are now outsourced, and it is uncommon for large organizations to employ many trainers, although they now tend to employ a number of HRD and management development specialists in a variety of fields.

In terms of how managers learn, the choice (of internal or external) is often immaterial. There are instances where someone with an external perspective can be more highly regarded or can wield a greater influence over managers. Equally, there are circumstances where only a colleague within the organization can be credible in understanding the details of a problem or situation. In many instances, the decision is likely to come down to cost. But it is worth bearing in mind that, for the learning manager, the experience is likely to feel very different in each case.

Indeed, one of the arguments advanced for self-managed learning is that traditional, formal management development effectively deskills managers, as it implicitly teaches them that they can find an expert for every problem, rather than learning how to solve problems from their own resources. The extensive use of external training providers may tacitly reinforce this message.

Most of the on-the-job techniques have to be implemented internally, although consultants may be able to help. Most of the off-the-job techniques can be implemented by either in-house trainers or external providers, although many of them require specialist input unlikely to be found within even the largest organizations. The final decision will be up to those involved, so it would be presumptuous for this book to dictate choices.

CHOOSING TECHNIQUES

The choice of management development techniques will sometimes not be an explicit choice at all – a technique will be determined almost by default, from the expectations of learning managers or external providers, or by dint of what is available or feasible within budgetary or other restrictions.

Most subjects – and management disciplines are no exception –

are intrinsically capable of being taught by a great variety of techniques. Other considerations will narrow the range of possible options, but there will almost always be a choice. The question for the management development professional is how to make that choice, or what criteria to use in arriving at a decision.

This book purports that one of the most important criteria is the correlation between a proposed technique and the preferred learning styles of the managers to be developed. Accordingly, there is some discussion under each technique of its learning style 'fit', and this information is gathered into a handy reference matrix in Appendix 2. There are other reasons (than learning style preferences) why managers may enjoy or dislike a technique and these are also highlighted. It can sometimes be difficult to get managers to accept the need for development, so it seems unnecessary to self-impose the handicap of using an unpopular technique to further alienate those managers.

On the constraints side, other important criteria are what may be feasible and affordable, so each technique is evaluated in terms of its practicality and cost-effectiveness, as well as being marked as either an individual or a group technique, and as either an on-the-job or an off-the-job technique.

EVALUATION

A final consideration will be how readily each technique lends itself to the evaluation that is needed by all management development.

Management development professionals will be familiar with the problem of justifying management development. Those who are involved in implementing management development measures are sometimes too close to see that, however inherently sound an initiative may be, it may be superfluous to the needs of the organization. It is an overriding business imperative that management development can demonstrate that it adds value, so it certainly helps if management development techniques lend themselves to the most commonly understood – and easy to implement – evaluation methods.

There are too many evaluation methods to do them justice in a brief survey here. Suffice to say that evaluation is not a bolt-on process at the end of a management development intervention, but should be part of the process from the earliest stages of needs analysis, solution generation and objective setting. This means it should be a factor to consider both in choosing a provider and in choosing a technique.

The preparations of management development professionals need to be informed by a corporate strategy, by a career development policy both for the organization and for individual managers, and by a perspective on the organization's competence needs. These factors, and how they are to be evaluated, will help determine an approach to making provision, and a choice of management development techniques.

Further reading

Craig, R (ed) (1996) *The ASTD Training & Development Handbook*, McGraw-Hill, New York

Rae, L (1999) *Using Evaluation in Training and Development*, Kogan Page, London

Whiddett, S and Hollyforde, S (1999) *The Competencies Handbook*, IPD, London

Web references

www.amanet.org
www.ist-mgt.org.uk

4

Courses and the classroom

COURSEWORK

Group-work	✔
Individual	✔

We begin with courses because they are probably the most common popular association with forms of management training and development: if asked how to develop a manager, many people will think first of a course. A textbook definition would be a meeting of learners, with a teacher, in a dedicated environment, for the express purpose of learning, following a curriculum – but there are exceptions even to this broad generalization, as we shall see. Some people prefer to call courses 'programmes', but this is an imprecise use of language.

The course as a technique is probably as old as learning itself – at least in any structured sense. We know of coursework undertaken by the ancient Greeks, and it was probably practised by even earlier civilizations.

People mean many different things by 'courses' nowadays, and the range provided in the marketplace is very large, from a short three-day course in supervisory management skills to universities' business degrees and postgraduate programmes such as the Master's in Business Administration (MBA). It is therefore insufficient to speak simply of courses in general without clarifying further, as the potential impact of various types of course will greatly vary.

THE CLASSROOM

What is invariably meant when people speak of courses is a classroom setting. There are exceptions, naturally, when a laboratory or workshop or other environment may be used. But although these may be important for other disciplines, they represent a very small minority when it comes to management development. If we take the classroom setting as a kind of 'lowest common denominator' of any course, we can then identify the various course types.

The term 'classroom' is deployed with reluctance, given its connotation of the schoolroom. Most classrooms used for management development, or indeed most adult education, are carpeted and soft-furnished, and generally more conducive to learning than ranks of desks and chairs. But 'classroom' is a more accurate description for development purposes than any of the alternatives – training room, boardroom or whatever.

HOW LONG IS A COURSE?

As to how long a course may be, like the piece of string, it depends how short it is.

Courses may be of any length, relatively short or long: the 'short' may be just a few hours – perhaps half a working day – while it is not uncommon for 'long' courses to last for more than two years. A full-time undergraduate honours degree in a management subject at a Scottish university lasts for four years.

Of the two case studies that follow, the first is an example of a typical 'long' course, a postgraduate programme at a business school, and lasts for about one year. The second is an example of a programme of 'short' courses, each about three days long, within a large, global organization.

Case Study 1 – Bass Brewers

Bass Brewers of Burton-upon-Trent is the second largest brewing concern in the UK, with around 7,000 employees, and is Britain's biggest exporter of beer. Its famous brands include the UK market-leading lager, Carling, and the top-selling imported beer in the USA, Bass Ale.

(At the time of writing, the sale of Bass Brewers by Bass plc to Interbrew of Belgium had been declared anticompetitive by the UK regulator. Interbrew, while challenging this ruling in the European courts, was seeking a buyer for Bass Brewers. This case relates to management development that began while Bass Brewers was still part of Bass plc, continued under Interbrew ownership and is intended to continue under the new owners.)

In 1993, Bass Brewers embarked on a major management development programme to provide their managers with knowledge, expertise and skills in the broad range of management disciplines. They chose to obtain a programme of courses from Nottingham Business School, part of Nottingham Trent University, where they had a close relationship, as sponsors of the University's Bass Management Centre.

Three course levels

Nottingham Business School (NBS) offers a suite of courses leading to management qualifications, in the form of an integrated management development programme. This consists of three course levels, each of which may be covered in one year's part-time study: the Certificate in Management (CM), Diploma in Management Studies (DMS) and Master's in Business Administration (MBA). This three-tier model of postgraduate-level management qualifications is common to many British universities. NBS designed a tailored version of the courses for Bass, including variations to course content and the assessment scheme, which would retain the same degree of academic rigour but also meet the specific needs of the corporate client.

The core course was the DMS, with the CM course providing a feeder to it, while some managers obtained exemption from the CM through an accreditation of prior learning (APL) process. A subsequent progression route to the MBA is left open for individual managers for whom it is relevant to pursue it. The DMS course lasts for one full academic year (about nine months).

Subjects and teaching methods

The Bass Brewers DMS consisted of the following subject modules:

- business policy/strategic management;
- structure and capability;
- financial resources;
- human resource management;
- change and implementation.

Each of these was taught via a one-week-long course. In addition, there were two work-based modules, one a team consultancy project and the other a management applications project. Each of these carried equal weight in assessment with the five taught modules. All seven modules carried five assessment credits, attainable through submission of a written assignment in each case. In addition, each manager had to compile a portfolio, consisting of a career profile (following a standard template), a learning contract for each module (agreed at the start of the course, between each manager and his/her manager at Bass) and a storyboard for each module, summarizing learning attainment and transfer to the workplace.

The taught modules consisted of a typical range of classroom-based activities: there were lectures, group discussions, syndicate work and case studies. These were supported by an extensive reading list of key textbooks, and learning guides in the form of a 'handbook' for each module, explaining key concepts and navigating paths through the reading.

At the time of writing, 100 managers had completed the course and attained the DMS, with further groups in progress. Gerry Topsom, Head of Management Development at Bass Brewers, thinks, 'Investing in business education is a good business deal. We get a good return on our investment by effectively increasing the intellectual capital in the business.'

Case Study 2 – The Department for International Development

The Department for International Development (DFID) is a relatively new UK government department of state, represented at Cabinet level by the Secretary of State for International Development. Founded in 1997, the Department was previously the Overseas Development Administration, part of the Foreign and Commonwealth Office. It employs around 2,000 staff in locations around the globe where the UK has, or had, an interest, such as the Commonwealth states. It divides its UK head-quarters between London and Scotland, and has overseas offices in many locations, notably the Caribbean, sub-Saharan Africa and Asia.

The Department's founding aims are elaborated in the 1997 White Paper *Eliminating World Poverty: A challenge for the 21st century* (an HMSO publication). The Department exists to tackle world poverty and to promote sustainable economic and social development in the developing countries of the world. More detailed information may be found on their Web site, www.dfid.gov.uk.

In the summer of 1999, on the initiative of Peter Farr, Head of Training and Development, the Department embarked upon a major management development programme on the theme of 'Managing Relationships', targeting staff worldwide. There was a general feeling that staff manage-ment needed improvement, and the experience of developing senior managers pointed to the advantages of a behavioural approach for all levels of management. The chosen approach was influenced by an exten-sive staff consultation on effective staff management, and the consonant pursuit of the Investors in People standard.

Deciding on short courses

Initially, a number of different delivery options were considered, but other course formats gave too much emphasis to intellectual development rather than the skills development and behavioural change that were needed. Techniques like open learning or action learning were seen as too long-winded to retain managers' commitment over a long period with no prospect of a qualification incentive (given the behavioural emphasis of the programme). The Department is task-focused, so a short course programme was deemed to offer more potential for behavioural improvement and increased personal confidence, while retaining the flexibility of local delivery at key points around the globe.

The majority of the short courses have been held in the UK, but other delivery points have included Nairobi, Harare, Pretoria, Bangkok, Kathmandu and Delhi.

Participating managers

The courses target staff from the Department's Band A, which includes senior managers up to but not including the Senior Civil Service, and Band B, which includes first-line and middle managers. A third participant group is Band C, which includes aspiring managers. The present schedule aims to complete the programme as originally envisaged by 2002, but that will represent just 75 per cent completion of a constantly shifting population of around 900–1,000 in Bands A and B, and a similar number in Band C – so the programme is expected to continue, although perhaps at a slower rate. Currently there are around three courses per month, or one per band.

Each course runs for two and a half days – three and a half for Band C participants – and is made up of a cohort from each discrete band; although the course content for bands A and B is identical (and Band C is similar) the questions for each band tend to be different, so separate cohorts make more sense. Each Band A cohort consists of 16 managers, while Bands B and C include 18 participants – these numbers were increased from, respectively, 12 and 15 (with a concomitant extra trainer to maintain the participant ratio) to account for high demand when no additional courses could be delivered within resource constraints. There are only so many courses that can be delivered at any given time, as they are facilitated by a small firm of external consultants, selected via a rigorous competitive tendering process.

The courses are effectively mandatory, without being explicitly so: there are links to further management development and an implied link to promotion, more overt in the case of progression from Band C to Band B. The courses are very popular and fully booked one year in advance. As is often the case, the managers in greatest need of the development tend to be those most reluctant to take part, but all will probably be levered into the programme eventually.

Course content

Under the general heading of 'Managing Relationships', the courses concentrate on behavioural skills, picking up on 360-degree feedback completed prior to the course. At the beginning of the programme, each participant's behaviour is analysed via a videotaped group session; then there is some flexibility and individual choice about what exactly to focus on. The courses are very participative, including little theoretical input, but rather are about establishing and maintaining good interpersonal skills. There is an optional one-day follow-up clinic, which helps evaluation and considers managers' opportunities for further development.

Within the Department's overall management development provision, the courses complement related programmes on negotiating and influencing skills, and managing diversity, and other courses addressing operational and procedural issues.

The courses are evaluated at a number of levels, from reaction sheets completed at the end of each course, to post-programme interviews with both managers and their staff. Because there is a practical difficulty arising from job movement of both managers and staff, and so no meaningful comparison with the pre-course work, 360-degree feedback is not used.

The courses themselves are held to be very sound, a good investment by the Department and effective in meeting their objectives.

SANDWICHES AND BLOCKS

A course's attendance mode may be full-time (including 'sandwich' courses or others taken on a break or secondment from work) or part-time. There are almost too many part-time options to list, but a brief classification would include day-release (attendance one day per week), block-release (several days, perhaps a week or more, at a time), evening classes and weekend classes.

Another key variable is the form of the coursework, such as a lecture to a large group (perhaps hundreds) or a small group discussion involving perhaps just a handful of managers. This may be subdivided into two variables: class size (the number of learners in a group) and the teaching/learning methods deployed. There are so many different methods that we shall deal with them in separate sections towards the end of this chapter.

A final course variable is whether it is certificated or not, ie whether assessment of the coursework leads to conferring qualifications on individuals. As the examples in Case Studies 1 and 2 illustrate, longer courses are more likely to be certificated, while shorter courses are less likely to lead to a qualification.

THEORY AND PRACTICE

Coursework in the classroom is especially suitable for learning anything with theoretical substance, such as management, and is suited to prolonged cerebral activity such as problem solving. It is also good for developing interpersonal communication and teamwork, including that essential management dimension, leadership. It is not so good at simulating real-life situations and, taken on its own, is no substitute for work experience in management development. This has led management development professionals to devise techniques that constitute a hybrid of the benefits of courses along with some more practical elements – as in open learning (see Chapter 5) and action learning (see Chapter 6).

One attempt to resolve the theory/practice dilemma is through competence-based courses. These are courses that seek to provide underpinning knowledge and understanding associated with management competences, and to advise and prepare managers to undergo competence-based assessment. But the course itself cannot provide the actual assessment, as that has to be carried out on the job.

Some managers have a particular aversion to courses. Not all managers are high flyers, and some have poor educational backgrounds – for many people, the associations of the classroom with their schooldays are overwhelmingly negative. Akin to this feeling is the sense that courses are by their nature too academic and remote from 'real life' and, in the most extreme expression, the notion that theory is too removed from practice to be valuable. Ideally, these views should be challenged, but it is often not worth trying to swim against this tide, when there may be short-term objectives or deadlines to meet. So for managers of these opinions, it may be better to choose other, more obviously practical, techniques.

COURSES, NOT PROGRAMMES

The term 'programme' is sometimes substituted for 'course'. A programme is broader and may indeed embrace courses, perhaps along with a combination of other techniques, but the substitution is rarely justified. The grander-sounding term does not aid clarity in this case – the term 'programme' is probably better suited to something like the open/flexible/distance learning schemes cited in the next chapter.

ONE TO ONE

The popular perception of a course is likely also to presume a group of participants – at least two and probably more – and our discussion thus far has followed this assumption. However, it is legitimate to speak of a course, in all of the senses described above, for the benefit of just one learner, in a tutor-learner ratio of one to one. This type of course is, in practice, much more rare, for the simple reason that it is so resource-intensive or expensive, but it is a technique sometimes deployed for senior managers in particular, perhaps in combination with coaching (see Chapter 6) or mentoring (see Chapter 6). Educationalists will argue that the learning dynamics of the one-to-one course are completely different from group learning, but the techniques as applied are virtually the same, albeit the tutor's approach will need to be very different.

TEACHING/LEARNING METHODS ON COURSES

Teaching/learning methods on courses include:

- lectures;
- seminars;
- small tutorial groups;
- workshops;

- T-groups;
- syndicates;
- case studies;
- projects;
- other exercises and activities.

Lectures

The most traditional, most old-fashioned and most didactic teaching technique is the lecture, a presentation that may be interrupted by questions and perhaps even some discussion, but is usually intended to be a one-way delivery. The lecture will often be supported by audio-visual aids, which may also be deployed to support most of the other techniques detailed in this section. Audio-visual aids may include emphasizing key points on a flip chart, blackboard or whiteboard, prepared celluloid slides presented via a carousel projector and screen, projection of written or printed matter via an episcope, or on transparencies via an overhead projector, or increasingly nowadays via a computer-based system, notably Microsoft's PowerPoint application, and of course the distribution of pre-printed support material or 'handouts'.

The lecture, even if delivered only in short bursts, is the cornerstone of most courses, and a powerful technique for getting across large amounts of theoretical information, which is especially useful where large numbers of managers (or would-be managers) are learning together. A lecture may comfortably be delivered to a hundred or more learners at a time. Its other strength is its ability to support complementary study of books or other materials, amplifying or explaining key points. Its weakness is its lack of involvement of the learners, limiting their learning potential: activists attending lectures are inclined to 'switch off'.

Seminars

Teaching to a smaller, more manageable, group is used to engender involvement through group discussion. The seminar is one form of this, the term usually implying a lesson for a smaller group that incorporates an informal lecture with questions and open discussion. The other connotation of 'seminar' is an academic context, as it is rarely encountered elsewhere, indeed the term 'academy' is a variant of this. But academics would not agree with this distinction, and so it is hard to differentiate a seminar from a small tutorial group in any meaningful way.

Small tutorial groups and workshops

Small tutorial groups can also be used to involve learning managers in exercises or other activities designed to simulate real work scenarios, thus adding a practical dimension to the theoretical inputs. Most short management development courses follow this model, whether delivered in-company or on an 'open' basis involving managers from several organizations. This is also the preferred model for periodic face-to-face tuition in open or flexible learning programmes (see Chapter 5). If the group meets occasionally, or perhaps only once, the session is often termed a workshop. There is no special term for when this service is provided for just one learner at a time – it will usually be referred to simply as a tutorial.

It is difficult to categorize small tutorial groups, seminars and workshops in the way we did with course modes, as the meanings of the terms overlap and are not used consistently. The duration of a single session may vary from around an hour to a full day; attendance will usually be for the entire duration; number of participants may vary from one to perhaps around 30; certification will not be applicable to this technique on its own. Broadly speaking, this technique has greater empathy (than a lecture) with the full range of learning style preferences.

T-groups

One specialized form worth mentioning is the T-group – also known as laboratory training or sensitivity training. T-groups are short, frequent sessions of no more than about two hours at a time, self-managed and typically unstructured, as the process is deemed to be more important than the content. The idea is to generate confusion and feelings of discomfort among group members, in order to stimulate self-searching and the formation of new values and behaviours.

T-groups are often used as a catalyst for broader organizational development initiatives, and share some of the same ground as emotional intelligence (although the technique is older than this concept). There is no great mystery about the 'T' – it stands, prosaically, for 'training'.

Syndicates

We can view the provision of face-to-face teaching/learning for such small groups as a continuum, with no distinct models recognized by any consensus. The only clear exception is when smaller groups are separated for simultaneous tackling of the same problem, or for tackling of different but related aspects of a problem. These smaller groups are termed syndicates, and this terminology is widely agreed, although some use the alternative names 'buzz groups' or 'breakout groups'.

Syndicates are useful for encouraging greater involvement and participation by more learners, for using competition as a motivational tool between syndicates, and as a time-saving measure when different syndicates can tackle different issues and then report back to a shared plenary session. A useful tip is to avoid letting one syndicate provide all the 'answers' in a plenary before others have had the chance to report.

Moving on, the exercises or activities used within sessions may be broken down into many categories. The most common are probably the case study and the project.

Case studies

The case study is an examination of events or situations (usually real-life) aimed at learning by analysing the detailed material, or posing and defining solutions for problems. Shorter versions are sometimes designated 'vignettes' or 'critical incidents' (see 'Critical incident analysis', later in this chapter).

Case study material is usually presented to managers in the form of a written brief, ranging from a couple of paragraphs for a short informal discussion, to some very sophisticated cases for more detailed analysis, perhaps stretching to several pages of text plus supporting accounts or statistical information. If managers have the opportunity to study the case in advance, then a lot of ideas and opinions can be generated and a lot of learning accomplished.

It is rare for the trainer to need to write up a case study (unless s/he wants to) as increasingly business schools, management development providers and other organizations publish interesting cases for widespread use. Some cases become well known and well worked, but most managers on a course are unlikely to have encountered a particular case before – and even if they have, there can be something new to learn, and the enterprising trainer will try to exploit the individual's previous knowledge.

Case studies may appeal most to theorists and perhaps reflectors.

Projects

These are also known as assignments, or as work-related projects, to distinguish them from work-based projects (see Chapter 6).

The project is usually a large-scale exercise, but leaving most of the process within learners' discretion. It can involve collecting and reporting data, and then offering conclusions and recommendations for improvement. Projects may be attempted by individuals or by teams, and the findings may be reported in a verbal presentation or in writing. An alternative application is as a means of generating evidence of competence for a portfolio (see Chapter 6).

The project is particularly suited to a longer course, since it can be broken down into a number of stages spread throughout the course: the trainer may try to reach agreement on a subject and terms of reference, and then provide continuous support during subsequent course meetings until the managers are ready to report. A more free-flowing structure (or lack of it) is also possible, testing managers' initiative. Projects also lend themselves naturally to marking schemes, and so can be a popular form of assessment (see Chapter 5).

Projects will appeal to activists, but there should also be plenty of scope for reflectors, theorists and pragmatists. They offer something for every learning style preference.

We shall return to the example of the project in Chapter 6, under consideration of on-the-job management development techniques.

Other exercises and activities

Other examples of exercises or activities that may be built into off-the-job management development are more esoteric, and too numerous to examine in any great detail here. As a general rule, the more participative ones tend to favour activists and pragmatists; the more passive techniques are more to the liking of reflectors and theorists. This author has come across the techniques outlined in the following sections (and there are bound to be many more).

Accelerated learning
Accelerated learning has been described as 'natural' learning, and indeed some of its advocates would describe most of the other techniques in this chapter as unnatural. It is a technique that ignores conventional wisdom about what works in teaching and learning, and instead looks at how the brain functions when constructing learning events and activities. Accelerated learning attempts to use the whole mind and the whole body in the learning process, and emphasizes creativity, involvement and discovery rather than didacticism.

Action maze
This is a very detailed group assignment, requiring considerable advance preparation by the tutor (although it may be possible to buy prepared packs). The assignment is to consider a given situation and select at various points from a number of alternative actions, effectively working through a 'maze', hence the name. This can be very helpful where the development content mirrors the technique, such as in decision making and decision trees.

Audio or video recording

This involves recording managers as they conduct a role-play, drama or simulation of any kind, in order then to play back and critically analyse their performances. It is a stronger technique in the visual medium, but can be cumbersome to set up and time-consuming, when training time is often scarce. Many trainers regard it as a very powerful technique to be able to give immediate feedback, reinforced by actual evidence, but a note of caution is that many managers are self-conscious about being recorded and dislike watching themselves on video playback. And trainers should be wary of showing videos to whole groups, as individuals can find this uncomfortable or even humiliating.

Brainstorming

A very common technique, brainstorming is used to generate ideas in a non-evaluative way in order to produce the maximum number of options before moving on to evaluate them. Typically, the trainer will explain to the group what to do, and then invite ideas around a given subject and write them up on a flip chart or whiteboard without comment. Only after every possible idea has been voiced and noted will the group move on to criticize and eliminate any ideas. This technique can be helpful in encouraging participation in the group by less extrovert individuals and in promoting an atmosphere of creativity. It may also assist the trainer in gauging the managers' levels of understanding.

Buberian dialogue

Named after Martin Buber, this is a kind of formal debate with constraining rules, where conflict is discouraged and the focus is on seeking agreement. This may be useful in promoting co-operation, teamwork and leadership through consensus building. Or it can serve as an illustration to a discussion of how people communicate.

Case history

Some people distinguish this technique from the more familiar case study, on the grounds that it is merely an account of events and circumstances in a case, presented to a group to highlight key facts, figures and interpretations. Whether to engage in a subsequent study of the case would be a separate technique, and arguably not the only use of the material from the case history. Some professions that regularly consider clients' cases find it useful to make this distinction.

Closure

This is a word game, where words are excluded from a passage of text and the managers are invited to fill in the missing words. The more words that are excluded, the harder the game becomes, while the easiest version provides an accompanying list of the missing words in scrambled order. This technique may be used to develop language and communication skills, or to test understanding of a concept (or both).

Creative dialogue

This is a form of discussion where the trainer hands control to the group. Initial questions or contentious statements are supplied to the managers, but without guidance as to what to do with them other than 'discuss'. Groups will often need to be given some parameters, such as a time-frame, or whether to break into smaller groups. The benefits of this technique are that more open and creative discussion should flow, and that managers should accept more responsibility. It may be particularly helpful in leadership and team-building training. The potential drawback is that the discussion becomes too unstructured and nothing much is achieved.

Critical incident analysis

The thinking behind this technique is that a greater understanding of an overall set of circumstances, or sequence of events, may be gleaned from detailed analysis of just one specific aspect, the so-called critical incident. It is a common problem-solving tool in some businesses, and may be used just like this in a development situation by a group of managers studying a case. Or it may be approached by inviting managers to contribute their own 'critical incidents', from their own experience, for discussion. An occasional variant, known as 'illuminative incident analysis', involves visual representations of the incident – for example, the managers may be asked to provide drawings on flip charts to illustrate their experiences.

Directed conversation

This is derived from the common practice of learners approaching their tutor informally at the end of a session, when more candid discussions sometimes take place. It is an attempt to include this type of discussion in a deliberate way within the session, to allow the whole group the benefit of it. Typically, the directed conversation will be initiated at a point when managers are more relaxed, perhaps just before the session formally starts or just after it formally ends or perhaps within a designated break, but when all of the group are present. The success of this technique will depend upon how adroitly it is handled by the tutor – the greater the informality, the higher the chance of a good discussion.

Drama

There is a growing awareness of the potential for drama in management development. A logical extension of role-playing (see below), short scripted plays – or even occasionally unscripted ones – can help managers literally act out situations they may have to deal with in real life. An especially useful method is to cast managers against type, opening up different perspectives to them. Specialized variations have sometimes been given specialist labels, including 'monodrama' (a single-person technique), 'psychodrama' (where the manager is invited to act out his/her conflicts) and 'sociodrama' (which is an unscripted version). The various options for introducing theatre into development offer innovation and excitement, which will have great appeal for many managers (but not all).

Encounter groups

Encounter groups are rather specialized forms of group-work derived from the science of psychology. Participants are encouraged to say what they really feel, in the belief that this is rarely possible in the real world. 'Basic encounter' is a simplified form developed by Carl Rogers and is sometimes named after him (Rogerian group or similar). 'Open encounter', developed by Will Schulz, tries to counter the impact of subconscious communication through body language. Both approaches may be helpful in developing better communication and change management skills, and basic encounter offers opportunities for testing the skills of a putative leader. For most trainers, the main drawback of encounter groups is that they require specialized study if they are to be implemented effectively.

Fish bowl exercise

This technique divides a group into two, with one sub-group undertaking a discussion or perhaps one of the other exercises described here, while the other sub-group observes from outside the 'fish bowl'. A subsequent debriefing session, involving the whole group, should expose differences in perception arising from participating or observing, but it can be a bit hit or miss.

Games
See Chapter 5.

In-tray exercise
The in-tray exercise provides a simulation of a real in-tray, containing various examples of administrative paperwork (correspondence etc) requiring a manager's attention. This helps develop decision-making and problem-solving skills, can show how a manager works under time pressure and can test the precision with which s/he attends to detail. For these reasons the technique is often used in recruitment and selection, but it may also be deployed within a development context when it need not be just an individual exercise. A group may be assigned to work through a full in-tray, adding a dimension of team working. Or individual group members may tackle the same in-trays simultaneously and then compare their responses. The problem pack, although ostensibly different in form, presents similar content to an in-tray, only this time to a whole group for open consideration of how to respond.

Jurisprudential framework

This obscure technique uses controversial issues to provoke debate – sometimes very contentious – on values and ethics. The idea is for managers to see through the emotionally charged conflicts to the underlying principles, facts and terms, and thence to learn to resolve such conflicts when they arise in real work situations. Not for the faint-hearted.

Lateral thinking

Arguably more an approach than a technique, lateral thinking is nonetheless an influential method, conceived in the 1960s by Edward de Bono. The idea is to look at problems or situations in an unorthodox or unconventional way – thinking 'laterally'. This can be expressed in many different exercises and activities, including games and controlled or constrained discussions. One of de Bono's own applications is the 'six thinking hats' discussion technique, which involves consciously adopting a narrow perspective, eg the 'black hat' for taking a dark, pessimistic view. The strength of lateral thinking techniques is in stimulating creativity and innovation.

Mind mapping

Invented by Tony Buzan, this technique is really for an individual to use, but may be deployed on a course to initiate managers in its use and allow them to compare with others. It is also possible for a group to produce a mind map. Essentially the idea is to write down all the ideas associated with a concept, in a controlled pattern – only one word or phrase allowed per line – but in the form of a sprawling diagram indicating, by lines, the relationships between different parts. This facilitates both an overview of a concept and an appreciation of the details, and helps stimulate creativity. Many individuals find it a powerful tool, but its use in group-work is probably limited.

Non-verbal exercise

This is almost a game, in that it involves managers in giving up their most common and conscious form of communication – the use of language in speech and writing. Various activities may be structured to involve communication by body language (mainly gestures and signs, but also facial and physical expression), drawing (but not writing), or perhaps acting (miming) or dancing. The main purpose of this technique is to teach communication skills, but it may also be useful in tackling issues around the management of diversity, such as working with the sensory-impaired. Care should be taken, as some managers may find it unsettling, and while this may be a positive thing it is also potentially destructive.

Panel discussion

This involves a group of 'experts' discussing an area of their expertise for the benefit of an audience, which enables a theoretical topic to be considered in great depth without relying on one individual. This, and the more imaginative setting, makes this technique potentially more effective than a straightforward lecture. However, the audience is fairly passive, unless the next, complementary, technique is also used.

Question time

Named for the eponymous television programme, some readers may recognize this as the 'brains trust', an older radio programme of a similar format. Another name for it is 'open forum'. Essentially, the idea is to use the panel discussion method with the addition of questions from the audience. This allows the managers to exert greater control over what, and how much, they learn, and promotes the useful skill of interrogating a subject.

Role-play and role-reversal

Role-play consists of the enactment of roles in a prescribed, artificial scenario where two or more learners are asked to suspend reality – and disbelief – and take on imaginary roles. A typical example is to enact a problem scenario at work in order to arrive at a resolution. This technique is often used in an attempt to shift attitudes and behaviour, and so is especially suited to issues around managing people and managing change. It is popular with trainers, as it can often be implemented with little or no resources, and even briefings on individuals' roles may be delivered *ad hoc*. Managers are sometimes reluctant to engage with the process, but usually find it rewarding. Role-reversal is a common variant where two protagonists in a role-play are asked to swap roles, or where a manager is asked to adopt a role contrary to his/her usual work role, such as a subordinate. More sophisticated role-plays become dramas (see above).

Storytelling

There is an increasing awareness of the value of storytelling as a technique. The theory is that people absorb information better in the form of an anecdote or tale. The gist of the technique, therefore, is to find ways to incorporate storytelling into coursework, either by the trainer telling stories or by eliciting stories from the participating managers. A more advanced application is to encourage managers to incorporate storytelling within their own management style. If implemented too rigidly, this technique runs the risk of alienating some learners, especially pragmatists, but most managers will warm to a more casual approach to sharing tales from their experiences.

Structured debate

A group discussion may be circumscribed by all sorts of rules, some of which may serve to focus discussion rather than act as a constraint. The structured debate is often set up as two opposing viewpoints, perhaps 'pro' and 'con' an idea, with timed speeches allowed for each side, questions to the speakers, open discussion and then concluding statements. It is even popular in some circles to follow UK parliamentary procedures. Structured debate works best where contributors have had the opportunity to prepare in advance; for impromptu debates, a more informal discussion is probably best.

Team teaching

This involves more than one trainer (usually two), and can be used in combination with most of the other techniques in this chapter, as it merely refers to the practice of more than one 'teacher', trainer or facilitator working with the same group. This can set a useful example in teaching teamwork and leadership, and it helps challenge conventional notions of the trainer's authority. Some trainers have a specific division of roles, where one trainer 'leads' and the other 'sweeps'. The other advantage is that a larger group can normally be handled than is possible with one trainer. One drawback is that two trainers are usually twice as expensive as one.

Videos
See Chapter 5.

Beyond this range of the more obvious techniques, there is probably no limit to the possibilities for facilitating courses, as the following case study demonstrates.

Case Study 3 – Michael Redfern

Michael Redfern lives and works in central Scotland, where he is the Employee Development Manager for Stirling Council. Between the cities of Edinburgh and Glasgow, central Scotland is mostly urban and industrial, but northwards, in the area around the town of Stirling, it is predominantly rural, and the low mountain ranges of the Ochils in the east and the Trossachs in the west point the way to the Highlands.

Stirling Council is a local government organization, overseen by elected councillors, which provides a broad range of services including schools, housing, roads infrastructure, social work and a great deal more. Michael is responsible for the Council's centralized employee development team that identifies and meets the development needs of around 4,500 employees in hundreds of different locations and types of premises – offices, schools, workshops, depots and yards.

Opening Pandora's Box

But Michael Redfern is a training manager with a difference, as a browse through some of his resources indicates. There's an overflowing box in his office that spills out sheets of poetry, pictures of fish, toy cars, a model of a head and the wheels off a baby's pram. Michael's courses convey the same initial impression of anarchy – but that is a misleading impression, as order emerges from the chaos, and his techniques prove highly effective.

Here are some examples of Michael's approach:

- A group of managers on a facilitation skills course were chall[...] devise 26 new facilitating techniques, each beginning with a [...] letter of the alphabet – and they did.
- As a problem-solving exercise, a group was invited to ut[...] Japanese haiku – a form of rhyme-less poetry with a rigid m[...] open up their creativity by looking at how they expressed something (within these confines) rather than what they said.
- As a communication exercise, he showed a videotaped scene from the British television soap opera, *Coronation Street*, but without the sound, and then invited the managers to script it, based on their observations of the action and the actors' body language, gestures, expressions, etc. Not only did the managers' script follow the real storyline, but some of the words and phrases they selected were precisely those used in the original dialogue.
- Samba drumming was used to teach leadership skills to senior managers, allowing expert samba drummers to pass on their skills in the way they considered best. This meant no drumming techniques were demonstrated – instead the managers were invited to clap, dance, shout and get into a rhythm, and then choose their drums and follow mouthed instructions (non-verbal) on how to get certain sounds from them, eg 'chugga chugga, chugga chugga, pow pow pow'. The lesson was in how to provide leadership, emphasizing a transforma-tional rather than transactional approach.

These are typical of the non-traditional coursework techniques he uses.

Rationalizing the irrational

Michael believes course facilitators can use anything to deliver a course – and that variety is much more than just a means of keeping learners awake. He advocates creativity in course techniques to spark creativity in the workplace. Sometimes the innovative use of techniques will inspire managers to innovate at work, while occasionally they will be able to use techniques directly that they have experienced on the course, such as brainstorming and mind mapping. This view derives from a strong belief that the best way to run a business, to look at an organization and to be a manager is to tap into people's creativity – using both the left and right sides of the brain – to unlock and develop their potential. Of course, you don't need to agree with this compelling belief to see merit in the type of techniques he uses.

It may come as no surprise that Michael was once an actor, and got into management development via work in which he used drama skills to help develop disadvantaged young people. He has also been heavily influenced by people like René Magritte, Salvador Dali and others in the surrealist movement, as is reflected in his choice of development techniques. In 20 years in training and development, he has established a reputation based on his consistent willingness to explore the boundaries of his role, using innovation and creativity to achieve tangible business benefits.

Michael Redfern would be happy to hear from others who are interested in this style of work. He may be contacted by e-mail at redfernm@stirling.gov.uk.

Further reading

Bee, F and Bee, R (1998) *Facilitation Skills*, CIPD, London

Heron, J (1999) *The Complete Facilitator's Handbook*, Kogan Page, London

Race, P and Smith, B (1995) *500 Tips for Trainers*, Kogan Page, London

Rae, L (1998) *Using Training Aids in Training and Development*, Kogan Page, London

Rae, L (1999) *Using Activities in Training and Development*, Kogan Page, London

5

Other off-the-job techniques

In this chapter we consider the management development techniques that are used mainly off the job. In some cases this categorization is clear cut and undisputed, but it is not always so straightforward and some techniques may be held by others to belong in the following chapter (and vice versa). No definitive claim is intended by their inclusion here – merely that it is possible for all these techniques to be used off the job.

Like the coursework in the preceding chapter, most of these techniques (except where indicated) are suitable for use both with an individual learner and with a group of learners.

The techniques that follow are:

- external events and visits;
- games;
- videos;
- psychometrics;
- outdoor development;
- open, flexible and distance learning;

- e-learning;
- resource-based learning;
- assessment techniques;
- development centres.

EXTERNAL EVENTS AND VISITS

Group-work	
Individual	✔

One of the simplest off-the-job techniques, closely related to sending a manager on a generic external course, is sending the manager to undergo some other experience. It's simple because there is so little control over what (if anything) the manager learns as to be almost a random act. Yet managers often learn a surprising amount from these experiences. The most obvious examples include:

- conferences (alternative names for conference-type events include seminar, symposium, presentation, convention, etc);
- exhibitions (or fairs, shows, displays, expositions, etc);
- benchmarking visits;
- exchange visits.

Conferences and exhibitions

Conferences are events at which a number of speakers make presentations on topics of interest to the audience, in the style of a course lecture (see Chapter 4) with audio-visual aids. Usually a conference will also include workshop sessions, in breakouts from the plenary, rather like course syndicates (see Chapter 4). Conferences typically cater for large numbers – many involve hundreds or even thousands of delegates – and take place over a day or two or three. They are usually staged in hotels or dedicated conference centres, hosted by industry or professional bodies, government organizations, or management development providers.

Exhibitions involve a large number of organizations that supply goods and services displaying their offerings on stands, presented in an array for the benefit of the exhibition visitors. Each stand normally consists of a backdrop, or a cubicle in a shell scheme, and a table holding the supplier's products (if they are tangible) and publicity and promotional materials, and is staffed by sales, promotions and customer service specialists. In order to stand out from the crowd, many exhibitors offer promotional gifts, free sweets, competitions and other inducements, and invest their stand designs with great creativity. Exhibitions are often held in conjunction with major conferences.

Benchmarking and exchanges

Benchmarking visits are essentially visits to other organizations to examine something special to their experience, usually good practice or innovation in some area. The term is borrowed from traditional crafts like carpentry, and implies raising one's organization's standards to that of the 'benchmark'. For example, when Scottish Power created open learning centres for all its sites in the 1990s, amounting to more than 40 such centres, many other organizations sent managers to visit the centres to see what transferable value they could find and take back.

Exchange visits amount to little more than reciprocal benchmarking visits. However, they tend to be less prescriptive and more free-ranging, perhaps because they are often arranged as much for public relations purposes as for management development.

Pros and cons

Theorists and reflectors enjoy conferences, perhaps exhibitions too, although they may appeal more to pragmatists seeking to interrogate exhibitors. All of these techniques may have superficial appeal for activists – appealing to their sense of 'doing something', but may disappoint in practice as they really offer a more theoretical experience. Organizations often favour these techniques because they appear relatively inexpensive, while being highly visible in business reports or reviews of activities – people can see that they're getting something for their money. But it may repay the effort to consider alternatives, since this inevitably raises the question of 'why' – always useful when considering the prospective impact of an outside event.

Some organizations ask managers to provide formal reports,

often in writing, after attending a conference or exhibition. This may be prompted by cynicism: sometimes a senior manager may suspect a subordinate manager of just looking for a day out of the office and so uses the report as a disincentive or, more positively, an attempt to ensure that some measurable value is gained (or, in the worst scenario, to protect him- or herself from any negative reaction further up the management line). A better approach may be to agree learning objectives or other goals prior to the event, and then review how far they were met afterwards.

Not wishing to strike too negative a note, it should be said that most managers have anecdotes about their experiences at conferences, and many of them are positive: attending external events helps networking (see Chapter 6) and provides memorable staging posts in an individual's career development. In order to get the most from it, it may be worth comparing this technique with the uses and difficulties inherent in certain, similar, on-the-job techniques, notably secondments (see Chapter 6) and discovery learning (see Chapter 6).

Case Study 4 – The American Society for Training and Development

When event organizers want to create something big to attract a mass audience, they hold a multifunctional event, combining the typical components of both a conference and an exhibition, perhaps with additional elements. In the UK, the largest such event concerned with management development is the annual conference and exhibition organized in Harrogate, North Yorkshire, in October by the Chartered Institute of Personnel and Development (CIPD), but even this is dwarfed by the largest event of its kind in the world.

The American Society for Training and Development (ASTD) is probably the world's leading training and development organization, and has a major interest in management development. Among its extensive range of activities, every year it organizes its International Conference and Exposition: this includes days of pre-conference workshops, a multi-layered conference (including subject-specific conferences within a conference) and a huge expo, or exhibition.

The event lasts for a week, attracts well over 10,000 delegates from more than 80 different countries, and includes sessions in Spanish as well as English. Keynote speakers in the conference sessions include some of the best-known names in management development in the world.

Interactive Conference Online

In 2001, for the first time, the event included an Interactive Conference Online in the weeks leading up to it. Speakers posted discussion leads on bulletin boards on all ASTD's virtual communities, and delegates were invited to join the discussions, ask questions of the speakers, submit tips and take part in online surveys.

Visitors to the ASTD event regularly report it as one of the most impressive conferences they have ever attended, a unique networking opportunity and an excellent source of information on up-to-date developments in training. Many recommend it highly as a way of developing senior managers, fast-trackers or managers with international responsibilities.

Web references

www.astd.org
www.cipd.co.uk

GAMES

Group-work	
Individual	✔

Games loom surprisingly large in the world of business management. Much thinking about business strategy is dominated by games theory, skills like negotiating are founded in game playing and games metaphors abound. There is a substantial, predominantly male, language of sports and games, applied so casually that many managers are unaware of it. Within this context, it makes sense that learning and development should draw (heavily) upon games.

We may speculate why it is that games are widely accepted as management tools, while play – in its wider sense – is usually not, and is seen as childish. It may be because of their association with adult (again, largely male) sports and games, or simply recognition of the essential likeness of competition in one field and the other.

Games justify separate consideration in this chapter, as they are typically free-standing resources, which although they may be deployed in the context of coursework are at least as frequently used independently. In their simplest form they are merely devices used within a course, requiring few or no resources: examples of these would be word games, which may be used as ice-breakers, or variations on children's games like consequences, which may be used to stimulate creativity or break up conventional thought patterns.

Then there are the more sophisticated games. Some may involve purely cerebral activity – board games or computer-based games come into this category. As information technology becomes so commonplace, the board games are increasingly anachronistic, while the computer-based ones blossom. Others may be more physical, requiring the use of unusual resources to accomplish tasks like building a tower or scaling an obstacle. The latter type may more often be deployed on a course, but the former are usually given to a manager or group of managers as a self-study resource.

Business simulations

Business simulations are almost a category of their own. These are, as their name suggests, artificial replications of business situations, in which managers have to manage simulated companies or parts of companies. They are often organized as competitions, with the winners being those with the highest share prices or profits. For example, Michelin run a worldwide competition based on Andromeda Training Incorporated's 'The Game of Income Outcome', an activity-based costing game. The use of computers has made it easier to manipulate large amounts of information, and so has made business simulations easier and cheaper to run, and more accessible.

Costs

The best games are often the simplest. It can be expensive to create any development resource, and games are no different: the economics are essentially the same, with bespoke production usually prohibitively expensive unless there is a big market with the possibility of substantial return. Buying an off-the-shelf game is a much less costly option, though less likely to be cost-effective, while the most primitive games, especially those used on courses, are likely to cost next to nothing, yet work disproportionately well.

Music

One specialist area consists of musical games. Music is an increasingly common learning tool, for much the same reasons as story-telling (see Chapter 4), and games are the easiest way to incorporate music into formal learning. Games often offer opportunities to provoke different senses (if the musical ear can be described as a different sense), and this can offer a handy mechanism for disrupting conventional thinking.

Fun

Games are fun, and so great motivators to learning. They can break up monotony in a lengthy development programme or help make a dry subject more interesting; they can enliven the learning experience. The other side of this coin is that they can seem frivolous and irrelevant – this makes them of doubtful value in any situation where managers are questioning the inherent value of the development they are undertaking. Indeed, in this sort of situation they can be counter-productive. Activists will enjoy them, but pragmatists may be sceptical unless they can see the value of this type of experimentation.

Case Study 5 – The Corporate Compendium

British Telecommunications plc (BT) is one of the largest companies in Europe, providing telecommunications services, including long-distance and international calls, to millions of customers. BT has a turnover in excess of £21 billion and employs around 136,000 people, mainly in its core, UK, operations.

When BT had a management development problem in its Northern Region, it hit upon a creative solution, and decided to get 45 first-line engineering managers to play games. BT involved an external training provider, Training Concepts, the UK licence holder for Prime Connexions Ltd, manufacturer of The Corporate Compendium.

The Corporate Compendium is a collection of three games, Corporate Planets, Corporate Service and Corporate Houses, providing multilevel business simulations. These are large-scale board games, which cover roughly the surface of a medium-sized boardroom table, include cards, movable pieces and other parts, and are accompanied by text-based workbooks. They are designed to be used by managers to act out, in a relatively relaxed setting, the problems they encounter in their everyday business lives and to formulate solutions. The games aim to offer practicality, sustainability and measurability.

Corporate Planets

Corporate Planets is a game about managing and developing people, to provide value-added outcomes for the business. It is based on a map of a solar system, where planets represent key areas of people management and development, and other cosmic elements influence people's behaviour and managers' decisions. One of the planned outcomes of the game is a people development plan, and for UK companies there is optional linkage to achieving Investors in People.

Corporate Service

Corporate Service is a game about designing and improving customer service systems and relationships, and developing a customer service culture. Managers compete in teams to construct towers built of bricks representing essential components of good organizational practice. A planned outcome of the game is a comprehensive design structure for world-class customer service, customizable to any organization.

Corporate Houses

Corporate Houses is a game about using the varying talents of different people in an organization to achieve business objectives. It emphasizes managing diversity and influencing relationships to 'put your house in order'. Managers compete to create a viable operational team, handling different individual styles and personalities to best effect. One of the outcomes is that they learn to make the most of their team resources, matching personalities to key tasks.

Making the games work

The games are enhanced by input from a facilitator. The messages are self-explanatory, but managers benefit further by using the game scenarios as a stimulant for discussion and individual consideration of how they compare to their previous experiences. In some cases, the games are linked to drama, with actors playing out the roles portrayed in the games.

In the BT case, the managers were engineers from the Newcastle area, recently promoted into managerial roles, with a coaching responsibility they found difficult to fulfil. They were not volunteers – they had been instructed to take this training; they didn't see the need for it and they definitely didn't want to play games.

However, once they got started, they rapidly engaged in the process and thoroughly enjoyed it. In post-training feedback they enthused about this innovative technique, praised its motivational qualities and spoke of its high learning value. Back at work, they transferred the lessons into practice, and now not only see the importance of coaching and other people development tools, but are also making a stronger contribution to the management of their business.

More information about The Corporate Compendium and other business simulations can be obtained from Alex Houston at Training Concepts (alex@trainingconcepts.co.uk).

Further reading

Elgood, C (ed) (1997) *Handbook of Management Games and Simulations*, Gower, Aldershot
Kroehnert, G (1992) *101 Training Games*, McGraw-Hill, New York

Web references

www.companyoccasions.ie
www.flyingstarship.com
www.prisim.com
www.riskybusiness.com

VIDEOS

Group-work	✔
Individual	✔

The presentation, analysis and discussion of videotaped scenarios can also be incorporated into coursework, but is often also deployed on its own, especially with managers. Its portability, allied to the fact that most homes have videocassette players, means managers can fit viewing a video into their hectic schedules as it suits them.

Use of humour

Managers looking at videos in the 80s and 90s were accustomed to seeing comic actors like John Cleese, best known as a film and television comedian, but also a hugely successful training video entrepreneur. His brand of showing the wrong way to do things, to hilarious effect, caught the *Zeitgeist* for a while. The formula was to show the wrong way and then the right way for each step, and underline it with a summary at the end.

The use of dramatic scenarios to simulate business problems on video, especially with the use of humour, peaked in the 1980s (when video technology was still fairly new). It was championed throughout the 1990s by a few niche suppliers, notably Cleese's Video Arts, but by the end of the decade was falling out of favour. The novelty of the technology has worn off, and the limitations of the technique have become more apparent.

DVD

Videotape was a popular technology for home entertainment, but is now being superseded by Digital Versatile Disks (DVD). As these are more flexible, they lend themselves readily to management development, but really represent no more than a storage medium, convenient for the domestic user, but virtually pointless in an organization with its own information technology network and server, its own Web site(s) and perhaps its own intranet.

The brevity of video's lifespan is demonstrated by the fact that a book published as recently as 1983, Andrej Huczynski's *Encyclopedia of Management Development Methods* (Gower), does not mention it but refers instead to 'films' – meaning 16-millimetre celluloid filmstrips, the previous technology. Films had been around since the 1940s: the technology existed even earlier, but it was during World War II that the US military realized the potential of the training film.

Pros and cons

Nevertheless, while the technology is still available, video is a useful technique for getting across a lot of theoretical content, as in a lecture but in a livelier way. And it can illustrate immediately with practical examples, unlike a lecture. Activists will not like this technique – recognizing the key weakness that it is too passive – but theorists and reflectors will appreciate it.

Other drawbacks are that it is expensive to produce a video unless the same content is to be taught repeatedly to a large number of managers over a period of time, and the much more common generic videos rarely have the same impact as bespoke ones. Taken on its own, the video is too one-dimensional to have any more impact on management development than reading a book – defenders of the technique will argue that it is not meant to be used on its own, but rather with guidance and tutorial support.

In some form, the use of moving images, reinforced with sound, will persist, but it is likely that the preferred medium of the future will be Web-enabled.

Case Study 6 – Video Arts' *Managing Problem People*

One of the most popular video-packs of the late 1990s was Video Arts' *Managing Problem People*, which is typical in form and design of this kind of product. Essentially, this example is a leadership development resource.

Described as a humorous drama, *Managing Problem People* features the acting talents of John Cleese, Emma Thompson, Stephen Fry, French and Saunders, and others in a series of short sketches that form a modular training programme. There are six sketches, each named for the type of problem subordinate they portray: 'Rule-bound Reggie', 'Bigmouth Billy', 'Moaning Minnie', 'Wimpy Wendy', 'Lazy Linda' and 'Silent Sam'. Altogether they amount to 96 minutes of video – or roughly feature-film length.

The complete pack includes the set of six videotapes, an accompanying booklet and a discussion guide. At the time of writing, the pack was available by direct purchase, but could also be rented, or each of its components could be bought separately. Its price – around £1,000 plus VAT and carriage in the UK – is fairly typical of products of this kind: cheaper options are available, but with any published resources you usually get what you pay for.

Web reference

www.videoarts.com

PSYCHOMETRICS

Group-work	
Individual	✔

Psychometrics (from the Greek *psychometria*, and conveying a sense of psychological measurement) has been an important aspect of human resource management for many years, dating back to its use by the Allied forces in the 1940s, but its primary focus has been on recruitment rather than development.

However, the administration, feedback and assessment of psychometric instruments can form a stand-alone off-the-job technique for management development. As a further alternative, the use of these instruments can be built into a course or a development centre (see later in the chapter). The most common forms of psychometric test are to measure personality type or aptitudes for particular kinds of task. For development purposes, the emphasis is more on the outcomes of tests, or candidate profiles. The trainer can use the profiles as a basis for discussion, to tease out development needs, promote self-awareness and encourage individual managers to review their learning; and the profiles may even be used in a similar way – with care and sensitivity – with groups.

Popular examples of psychometric instruments are:

- 16PF ('PF' stands for 'personality factors');
- the OPQ or Occupational Personality Questionnaire;
- the Myers-Briggs Type Indicator (MBTI);
- Meredith Belbin's team role questionnaire.

Among others that may be particularly relevant to management development are David Kolb's learning style inventory and Richard Boyatzkis and Daniel Goleman's emotional competency inventory. And market-leading suppliers Saville and Holdsworth publish 'Advanced Managerial Tests', addressing verbal application, numerical reasoning, verbal analysis and numerical analysis.

Pros and cons

One criticism of psychometric instruments is that managers are often suspicious of them, and try to second-guess their logic and intentions. This means the instruments have to be long and complex by way of disguise, and have to be scored by experts. In response, some suppliers offer self-assessment questionnaires purely for personal development, supported by the rationale that people will be honest with themselves.

There is also some debate about how to define and classify psychometric instruments. There is a huge variety of products on the market, including those mentioned above, plus interest inventories, ability tests and various tests of competence (eg McBer and Company's Managerial Competency Questionnaire). Some would classify all of these separately from psychometric tests, but their uses and applications are very alike – they are all development tools that aim to measure an aspect of the individual person.

Like games, videos and books, these can be useful among a range of techniques deployed in a programme, but are limited development tools on their own. Theorists and reflectors will appreciate them best, and pragmatists may well too, but some activists may be hostile.

As with other resources, the costs of buying off-the-shelf instruments are low, but the costs of buying expert support, notably interpretation of results, and advice and counselling of managers, can be as high as with other forms of consultancy.

Case Study 7 – Baker Hughes

Baker Hughes Incorporated of Houston, Texas, is one of the world's largest oilfield service companies, with annual revenues of $4.5 billion and around 26,000 employees. One of its six main divisions is Baker Hughes INTEQ, which provides advanced drilling technologies and services that deliver efficiency and precise well placement.

Dave Sherrit is worldwide Employee Development Manager for Baker Hughes INTEQ and, among other management development initiatives, he personally administers the Myers-Briggs Type Indicator (MBTI). In a year, he provides one-to-one feedback to around 50 managers at various levels.

The choice of instrument

The MBTI is used because it lends itself to development rather than assessment for selection, and it has the advantage of being well known in both the USA and the UK. Also, Dave Sherrit considers that it empowers managers to make active use of the data: many tools produce long, narrative reports, but are (deliberately) opaque about how they work or the theories behind them – MBTI takes a more open approach.

Within Baker Hughes, the tool is used to develop individuals (and occasionally teams) by extending their awareness of psychological type. The main applications of this are the provision of information supporting feedback and interpretation of 360-degree reports, and the support of career management through helping individuals strengthen their understanding of themselves and their interpersonal relationships.

Using the MBTI

The process with each manager is to have an initial one-to-one discussion to clarify goals and the context for using the information yielded by the test. Then the manager spends 25 to 40 minutes completing the test. The feedback session takes place, usually over one to two hours, although it sometimes takes longer, at any time from immediately after the test to within a couple of weeks, depending upon how it suits the manager involved. The feedback takes longest because it is the most important part of the process.

The initial discussion covers not just goals, but confidentiality, ethics, origin and history of the tool, what type is and means, and the dichotomies inherent in the tool. Dave Sherrit favours getting the manager to identify his/her type first (the self-assessed type) before taking the test and seeing what it reveals (the self-reported type).

In the feedback or debrief, he helps guide the manager to deciding his/her 'best fit' type – a combination of the self-assessed and self-reported. Sherrit maintains that the real benefits come when you begin to discuss the dynamics of type and look at how type is applied in certain situations. This is because he sees the tool not merely as a simple inventory, but rather as a lever for enabling behavioural change. The feedback can often lead to a follow-up session, days or weeks later, when the manager has had a chance to consider how s/he has applied the lessons learnt.

Weighing it all up

Baker Hughes have found this approach invaluable, and an extremely cost-effective form of management development. Since an initial investment in the registration and training of Dave Sherrit, the only costs apart from managers' time have been the nominal sums required to purchase copies of the instrument. In return, Baker Hughes have added another dimension to the range of development techniques they offer their managers, and demonstrated substantial commitment to the development of individuals. On the debit side, Sherrit acknowledges that it is difficult to track and measure real benefits to the organization, although he feels confident the inevitable improvements in managerial behaviour must have an overall positive effect.

One pitfall Baker Hughes have avoided is rolling out MBTI as a major development initiative in its own right, adopting instead a more low-key approach. Their method has been to use this psychometric instrument as a complement to the range of other management development techniques they offer. Dave Sherrit is certain it will be an important tool in his kitbag for many years to come.

Further reading

Lewis, G and Crozier, G (1999) *Psychometric Testing*, Hodder & Stoughton, London
Toplis, J *et al* (ed) (1997) *Psychological Testing: A manager's guide*, IPD, London

OUTDOOR DEVELOPMENT

Group-work	✔
Individual	

This is also known as adventure training or similar, and includes Outward Bound.

There is one outstanding example of a kind of management development course that takes place outside the classroom, and that is outdoor development. The term is unfortunately not very clear in conveying its meaning, and is probably better understood by many of us via the brand-name association of Outward Bound. Essentially the idea is to use the environment of the outdoors to teach management subjects like teamwork and leadership, and to develop desirable managerial attributes like endurance, determination, focus, decisiveness and clear communication.

Entrepreneurs as frontiersmen?

Outdoor development originated in the UK, which remains the heartland of provision, and rose to prominence in the 1980s amid a drive to encourage enterprise in general and entrepreneurship in particular, as there seemed to be a concept-fit with 'rugged individualism'. Its earlier history, in common with a number of techniques now popular, is that it was used extensively in the military as an aid to officer selection in the Second World War. Nowadays, providers are often keen to distance themselves from the stereotype of the 'commando course'.

In the last 20 years, specialist providers such as Outward Bound have found that two significant, if dissimilar, markets are: 1) youth trainees on government-funded schemes, along with other funding-dependent, often socially disadvantaged groups; and 2) managers funded by corporate clients.

Some provider networks have developed throughout the world. Outward Bound operates a franchise system, while Brathay Hall Trust has partnerships with Mida in Italy, Stucki in

Switzerland, Expérientiel in France, Outdoor Unlimited Training in Germany, Group Egor Recursos Humanos in Portugal, Innotiim in Finland, Technikon Pretoria in South Africa, Outbound Foundation in India and Excell Mountaincraft in Australia, among others.

Pros and cons

The strength of these programmes – and their appeal for managers – is their novel and, for some, enjoyable setting. Their weaknesses lie in the extent to which they depend upon physical or sporting prowess not needed by managers in their real jobs, and the lack of relevance in transferring the skills applications and the learning outcomes to the manager's workplace. This is definitely one for the activists, but in best practice also for reflectors, as Case Study 8 illustrates.

Outdoor development scores well as a team-building technique, and can be tailored to stretch the leadership experience of a select few managers by controlling who does what. If used sparingly, it certainly offers variety, but it is no substitute for the more established methods of imparting knowledge, such as traditional coursework, the use of resources or open learning. Imaginative providers of outdoor development insist on combining sessions in the outdoors with more traditional techniques in an indoor setting. They also make a great effort to relate the outdoor experiences back to the workplace, and to make connections with competence schemes. A kind of quality assurance document is available in the form of a guide to best practice, issued by the Development Training Users Trust.

There are now so many providers that the market seems to be constantly oversupplied. This means there is ample choice of (slightly) tailored programmes to suit every corporate budget, making this an attractive option when costing alternatives. One contributory factor to this is the low-cost accommodation invariably built in as part of the 'experience' – management development professionals need to bear in mind that those managers who enjoy their creature comforts may react badly to this.

Case Study 8 – Oki

Oki Electric Industry Company Limited was founded in Japan in 1881 by Kibataro Oki. The company manufactures and markets telecommunications systems, information processing systems and electronic devices. It has a turnover in excess of ¥67,000 million, and employs more than 21,000 people worldwide.

When Oki began production in the UK, they found employees recruited from traditional British manufacturing industries brought with them a different set of values from those emphasized in Japanese business culture. Oki spelt out their core values as the promotion of teamwork, respect for all team members, constant seeking of improvements, being flexible and keeping promises. They resolved to develop their new and existing manufacturing team leaders to be positive role models of the Oki values.

Short courses proved to be effective in developing knowledge and skills, but something more profound was needed to change team leaders' attitudes and beliefs. The solution was a year-long programme, focusing on personal development and including a cyclical review mechanism, kick-started by a challenging residential period, including use of the outdoor environment. Oki contracted Terra Nova Training, a provider with a strong sense of positioning outdoor management development in a broader context.

Using the outdoor environment

The ropes and boards, the rafting and abseiling, the climbing and orienteering, all play a part in getting managers to work together. But more than this, it is the physical and emotional impact of the countryside, its beauty and tranquillity, but also its harshness, that stimulate the senses and provide a context for reflection on personal behaviour, motivation and interaction with others. As Phil Maughan, Partner in Terra Nova, puts it:

> Some people see the outdoors as a macho environment. I see the opposite. Its unfamiliarity in many ways replicates the uncertainty many people experience in today's fast moving workplace, where support and empathy are critical to both leaders and teams. So the outdoors is a great place to practise and develop these behaviours. The physical contrast between the outdoors and the regular workplace also offers some valuable comparisons. Some of our behaviours might stay just the same despite the new environment, indicating quite deep-seated norms. Other behaviours may change, indicating

that not everything is set in stone, and that we can change some things if we choose. So the outdoors can stimulate a lot of personal learning, about ourselves and our relationships with others. But it also needs effective facilitation. In inexperienced or macho hands, its power can be misunderstood or misused.

An integrated programme

Terra Nova designed and implemented a programme involving the team leaders, their line managers, Oki's HR function and Terra Nova trainers. The team leaders identified their individual development needs using a competence questionnaire linked to the Oki values, and drew up personal development plans. Then the four-day residential phase tested the accuracy of their plans, through the challenge, uncertainty and heightened intensity of the outdoors. Team leaders worked with their line managers to review progress, and had regular interviews also involving an Oki HR manager and a Terra Nova trainer.

This approach has proved very successful, and has yielded significant measurable benefits. There have been improvements in productivity and waste management on the assembly lines of the participating team leaders, the programme has helped develop a pool of talent to aid succession planning and senior management is satisfied that the right values are becoming firmly embedded.

The programme has been repeated five times, with seven or eight team leaders in each case, and direct costs have run to around £75,000. In 1996, it was recognized by winning a National Training Award.

Further reading

Bank, J (1994) *Outdoor Development for Managers*, Gower, Aldershot
Krouwel, B and Goodwill, S (1994) *Management Development Outdoors*, Kogan Page, London

Web references

www.brathay.co.uk
www.kurthahn.org
www.outwardbound.org
www.reviewing.co.uk
www.terranovatraining.co.uk

OPEN, FLEXIBLE AND DISTANCE LEARNING

Group-work	✔
Individual	✔

These kinds of learning are also known as 'asynchronous' learning, correspondence courses, flexistudy or variations, sometimes proprietary, on this theme.

Correspondence courses

The origins of this strand lie in the correspondence course, which was essentially a course without the classroom, and required little or no attendance. 'Distance learning' is the more common term for this now, since communication is not just by correspondence, but by a variety of other means: in the sense of 'exchange of letters' it is often not by correspondence at all.

Distance learning can now be conducted by many technologies, including post, telephone, fax, radio and television broadcasts, electronic whiteboard, tele-conferencing, video-conferencing, e-mail, intranet and extranet discussion groups, and branded Web-based systems such as Lotus Learning Space, Blackboard and Docent. The best of these media allow for two-way communication: broadcasting, for example, is usually just a one-way process, but the newer technologies allow tutors and learners to interact, with learners offering inputs that assist not just their own learning but that of other learners in their group.

Correspondence courses date back centuries, certainly to classical times, at least in one-to-one provision. Correspondence schools became common in Britain and the United States in the 19th century, and persist to this day. So ingrained is the notion that some providers retain the terminology, despite having moved on in terms of technology – one successful global provider is the International Correspondence School (ICS).

Programmed learning

Another source of this technique is programmed learning, which paved the way for the design of the interactive open learning workbook. This term has become virtually defunct as some people resented the connotation of 'robotizing' managers. But the concept survives: the idea that learners follow a set programme of self-study is the cornerstone of both the open learning workbook and computer-based training (sometimes abbreviated to CBT).

Taking to the air

An open learning revolution took place in Britain in the 1960s, when two new institutions emerged. One was the National Extension College, which became a model for open learning providers throughout the world and, in 1980s Britain, first the Open Tech programme and then the Open College. The other was the Open University, initially conceived as 'the university of the air', which rapidly became the foremost distance learning provider in the world, a status it retains to this day.

The emphasis on broadcasting proved misplaced. Television helped publicize the Open University, but was never central to its delivery of course content. However, the constant presence of the OU logo on UK television screens encouraged the belief that broadcasts were the main way of learning. When the UK government conceived of the Open College in the 1980s, it initially launched it as 'the college of the air'. More recent technological developments have exposed the limitation of broadcasting as insufficiently interactive.

Britain has led the world in open learning since the 1960s. Not surprisingly, distance learning has developed most in countries where people are spread far apart, such as in North America and Australia. Open learning, by contrast, has tended to flourish where educationalists have focused on social concerns, in Western Europe – especially Scandinavia – and in the former British Commonwealth.

Changing corporate thinking

Within the context of corporate training and development, it was once the case that management trainers needed only some basic tools, such as the classroom-based techniques listed in the section on coursework, but two things have changed this. One is the revolutionary thinking of the last 40 years around open learning, and the other is the phenomenal innovation of information and communications technology. The latter has made possible e-learning (see later in the chapter).

Distinguishing open, flexible and distance learning

Distance learning lends itself to disciplines with a theoretical rather than a practical emphasis, and so is well suited to management development. However, as distance learning means limited opportunity for contact with tutors or other learners, it is constrained in its usefulness for developing interpersonal communication skills, which is one important dimension of management development.

The terms 'open learning' and 'flexible learning' are often confused with 'distance learning' or taken to mean the same thing. Both are approaches that emphasize certain benefits – openness or flexibility – that usually depend on distance learning technologies. Open learning may be seen to represent a marriage of some elements of distance learning with action learning (see Chapter 6).

One of the paradoxes of open learning is that it has a strong on-the-job focus, despite being ostensibly one of the most off-the-job techniques. Managers using a self-study workbook will certainly need to spend time in a library or study, or at home, reading it like a textbook. But they will also need to take it in to work, try out activities in the workplace and test assumptions in their own managerial dealings. Some would point to this as one of the technique's greatest strengths.

Open learning has also been characterized as 'learning the Martini way', invoking the long-running Martini advertising slogan of 'anytime, anyplace, anywhere'. This helps emphasize the breadth of the technique, mixing distance learning methods with whatever other inputs help make the learning more 'open' to its intended audience, such as with a mixture of self-study, tuition at a distance and some periodic face-to-face work.

Open access

The Open University, essentially a distance learning provider, was conceived with the intention of opening access to higher education, and typifies an open learning approach. Openness has the virtue of drawing in learners who might otherwise be unable to participate: this may be a key consideration for would-be managers, who may lack the opportunity to attend courses aimed at identifying and developing managerial potential. Opening up management development is thus about overcoming the obstacles to people taking part in a programme.

Therefore, open learning is about an open-minded approach to programme design, open access for participants, an open philosophy regarding delivery methods and sometimes even an open agenda.

Flexibility

Flexible learning emphasizes the benefits of flexibility both to the learning manager and to his/her employer. The significant flexibilities are opportunity to study at whatever time, in whatever place and at whatever pace suit the manager and his/her employer. These were once the key benefits claimed for open learning until it became apparent that openness and flexibility were two separate, albeit complementary, categories. It is not difficult to see that flexibilities can be obtained by other means than open or distance learning.

Flexible learning can be one of the most convenient ways to develop managers against a competence framework. In a competence programme, where managers already know and can already do most of what is required of them, each manager is likely to have different development needs or, at least, the same needs at different times from his/her colleagues. Flexible learning is ideal for filling these gaps.

Corporate universities

Corporate universities represent perhaps the most sophisticated flexible learning technique. Essentially the idea is that the organization centrally organizes all of its management development, brands it and markets it as a corporate university: some see this as the ultimate expression of a learning organization. McDonald's, with their 'hamburger university', were among the first to use this sort of language, although their example is more of an entry-level training school than a business school for their managers. Case Study 10 provides a more typical example. The development of Web-based learning technology has massively increased the potential for this concept.

Overall, open, flexible and distance learning represent a rich vein for management development, opening up a number of possibilities for combining other approaches and techniques. Through them, there will be something to be found for every preferred learning style.

Case Study 9 – Standard Chartered Bank

Standard Chartered Bank (SCB) traces its roots back to the mid-19th century, with origins in India, China, Australia and South Africa. It merged into its present form in 1969, and today describes itself as an 'emerging markets bank', with core businesses in consumer banking, corporate and institutional banking, and treasury. SCB employs over 33,000 people in 740 offices in more than 50 countries worldwide, with its largest presences in Hong Kong, Singapore and Malaysia.

Getting started

In 1998, SCB embarked upon a global business leadership development programme, which aimed to develop management skills in its leaders and future leaders. This was part of a wider strategy of preparing for growth, as the bank has recently pursued an aggressive acquisition agenda. The programme links to a major talent management initiative, targeting selectively those managers considered as having high potential within the bank. At the time of writing, around 2,500 managers have been through the programme, which is ongoing: high staff turnover in Asia, especially of managers, means the target population is constantly changing, and the bank considers the programme may be needed indefinitely.

Managers from all levels take part, from supervisor or team leader to all but the most senior bands of management, and from all over the world. Face-to-face tutorial support is provided worldwide and, although the programme is delivered in English, there is some scope for translation for those whose first language is not English.

Programme design

The programme is delivered by distance learning, with workshop support at various locations. This approach was chosen partly because it seemed impossible for managers to take sufficient time off to attend classes for a traditional course, but also to tackle some cultural issues. The bank felt it had a rather paternalistic style, particularly in Asian countries, where managers deferred decisions up the line, and so it sought a management development technique involving self-study to encourage managers to take the initiative and accept responsibility for themselves. It was also an effective means of ensuring relatively consistent delivery on a global scale, and was demonstrably a more cost-effective option for the bank's far-flung operations.

SCB conducted a competitive tendering process and selected a supplier that could develop and publish effective learning materials, and provide a distance learning delivery infrastructure worldwide. The programme had to have its own integrity, lead to certification (which SCB managers value highly) and comply with the bank's extant core competences:

- strategic perspective;
- business goal management;
- risk management;
- team orientation and people management;
- multicultural awareness;
- networking;
- change agent;
- customer focus;
- information systems management.

This led to the creation of a modular distance learning programme at two levels. The first level corresponds to a discrete level of SCB competences (level 3) and to the award of a postgraduate-level Certificate in Management from a UK university; the second level corresponds to SCB core competence level 4 and to the award of a postgraduate Diploma in Management. There are six modules at each level. The Certificate modules are:

■ You and the Business;
■ Managing Information;
■ Building Networks and Relationships;
■ Managing Business Goals and Risk;
■ Maximizing Team Performance;
■ Focusing on your Customers.

The Diploma modules are:

■ Business Goal Orientation;
■ Managing Information and Advanced Decision Making;
■ Risk Management;
■ Achieving Results with People;
■ Customer Orientation;
■ Strategy and Change.

Some managers attempt just one module at a time, but most go on to complete the full programme. Each module includes a self-study work-book, distance tuition by telephone and to some extent e-mail, and attendance at a one-day workshop. Each module is assessed by a written report on a work-based assignment, which requires the manager to investigate an aspect of his/her work, generate options for change and make recommendations for improvement. The assignments work best where the issues are current and relevant, and where there is clear support and sponsorship from managers' managers. To complete a full Certificate or Diploma, each manager also has to undertake a more substantial, broad-based project, exploring linkages between the modules.

Programme features

Managers spend around six to eight hours per week studying the work-books, which focus on best practice and feature well-known companies from around the world, including a balance between those from the financial services sector and those beyond. The Certificate programme takes around 12 months to complete and the Diploma around 15 months. For those who have completed the Diploma and wish to go further, there is a clear progression route to an MBA, via a further 12 to 18 months' study (part-time or distance learning).

The programme is supported by a number of other useful features. There is a learning contract, which every manager fills out at the outset, in collaboration with his/her manager and signed by both of them: this is also communicated to the external tutor and an HR relationship manager from within SCB. There is a network of informal study groups. There is a formal mentoring network, led by managers who were past programme participants. And there is a supplementary workbook, which looks at the context of the programme in the bank, learning styles and skills, using line managers and other support, and maximizing the effectiveness of assignments.

Just prior to getting started, there is a compulsory two-day induction workshop, which covers orientation to the programme and attempts to introduce and explain everything. Post-programme evaluation weighs managers' opinions of the workbooks, tutors and assignments, among other things.

Taking stock

Overall investment in the programme has been substantial: each division has to contribute over US $4,000 towards each participating manager, and that just covers costs in what is now an ongoing multimillion dollar initiative. But it is regarded as money well spent. Lessons learnt from the programme include the need for good service level agreements with suppliers, making roles and responsibilities clear, and the importance of making managers more responsible and willing to act on their own initiatives.

Paula Hindes, Head of Global Management Development Training, based in Hong Kong, believes that 'lots of training events are a waste of money' but she is a firm believer in the effectiveness of this distance learning programme, claiming 'this is the best learning process the bank has'.

Case Study 10 – Motorola University

Motorola Incorporated is one of the world's largest electronics concerns, with leading market positions in mobile phones and related devices, cable television systems, semiconductors and electronic systems for a variety of applications. With headquarters in Illinois, USA, the company employs around 120,000 people in 68 countries worldwide and dates its roots back to 1920. Its education and training – and management development – efforts are built on a philosophy of 'constant respect for people'.

A new approach

In 1989, the company established Motorola University as a global service in order to provide a more holistic approach to learning for their employees ('associates') and to build a community of learning in the sense of the Latin *universitas*. It now invests as much in creating knowledge as in providing training, within the context of being the strategic learning organization for Motorola and a catalyst for organizational change.

Motorola University describes its mission as:

- to be an agent of change;
- to provide training, education and development to every Motorola associate worldwide;
- to be part of the value-added chain of doing business with Motorola;
- to be the protector and conveyor of ethics, values and history of Motorola to all associates.

The structure of Motorola University includes a learning development and research arm, which designs and develops learning interventions through three colleges, Leadership and Transcultural Studies, Technology, and Emerging Markets, customized learning design, access to a vast library of books and other resources, and a virtual area. There are also divisions handling consulting and training services to Motorola suppliers and customers, lifelong learning for the wider community through Education Systems Alliances, and a major quality and excellence initiative called Six Sigma Black Belt.

Through the leadership college, a huge variety of initiatives is rolled out to managers at three broad levels distinguished within the company: new or first-line managers, middle managers and executives. One guiding principle is that only data-driven programmes should be implemented, or that needs should be justified by evidence, as distinct from the whims of powerful senior individuals. This yields high-impact programmes with an emphasis on processes rather than courses, of which the following are examples:

■ *Motorola Management Foundation Programme.* This is a new-manager programme. It starts with a motivational event built around Motorola's own bespoke leadership competences, followed by an assessment conducted online, which directs managers into a range of 40 modules delivered online to the desktop. It ends with a 'capstone' event, in which managers revisit their original groups to share feedback. The whole process lasts around 18 months.

■ *Achieving Results Through People.* This is a middle-manager programme, consisting largely of a refresher course on management theory, which some Motorola trainers consider rather dull, but the participating managers find stimulating and enjoyable. The format is essentially the sharing of stories from managers' real experiences, linked to the theoretical concepts.

■ *Leadership Institute.* This is the cornerstone leadership programme for managers coming to terms with what leadership really means, based on the principles of Neuro-Linguistic Programming. After a conventional opening, the managers are disturbed to find they are expected to determine the content of the rest of the programme. The format thence is for half of the managers to attend each module, and then to teach it to the other half.

■ *Executive development.* The focus for the most senior executives is more targeted, and consists largely of action learning programmes of a strategic nature. These tend to lead into real initiatives, with new jobs being created and new corporate systems implemented as a direct outcome of these programmes. One recent example has been work on the 'war for talent' and the need to make a differential training investment.

These examples help illustrate the overall approach. Motorola University is a permanent dedicated resource available to all managers and other staff of Motorola – and a still broader audience – throughout the world.

Further reading

Chute, A *et al* (ed) (1999) *The McGraw-Hill Handbook of Distance Learning*, McGraw-Hill, New York

Collis, B and Moonen, J (2001) *Flexible Learning in a Digital World*, Kogan Page, London

Paine, N (ed) (1988) *Open Learning in Transition*, National Extension College, Cambridge

E-LEARNING

Group-work	✔
Individual	✔

E-learning is also sometimes referred to as 'online learning'. Some people use e-learning in a wider context, meaning all IT-based learning and referring to any learning stored in an electronic medium, including CD ROMs and even computer-based training held on floppy disks. In this book some of these are included under the heading of resource-based learning, and only those techniques that fall within the sphere of electronic communication are included here.

E-learning is probably the single most exciting new technique in this book, not least because of its potential to open up still newer methodologies such as virtual reality. It is also becoming extremely popular: the value of the market for e-learning in Europe alone is estimated to grow from a little over £200 million in 2000 to nearly £3 billion by 2005. On a cautionary note, these figures refer to all training and development, and it is clear that management development has been slower to be adopted in this medium.

Some would argue that it represents old wine in new bottles insofar as it amounts to distance learning carried by a new medium. This may be strictly accurate, but ignores the emotional impact of the new technology and the consequent potential for a sea change in how managers access learning.

A technological revolution

Perhaps the most far-reaching consequences of new technology developments in the last 100 years are those associated with telecommunications. E-learning is part of this, and the logical extension of a range of now commonplace business tools that includes tele-conferencing, video-conferencing, e-mail and e-commerce applications.

Managers interested in this kind of learning can now use not just desktop and laptop computers with modems, but wireless application protocol (WAP) mobile telephones and other hand-held devices – some people are starting to use the term 'm-learning' ('m' for mobile) to refer to wireless access. Digital broadcasting means domestic television sets are now capable of Internet access and interactivity. In-car devices are also developing. There is an explosion of means whereby a manager can access learning.

Essentially e-learning consists of the provision of learning content and support through e-mail and the more sophisticated options made available by the Internet, extranets and intranets. This means that managers can access (from any of the hardware cited above) a range of learning input, including not just text and accompanying photography and artwork, but video images and interactive opportunities in all these modes. The only limitations of this medium are cable bandwidth, which currently limits the amount of video or other complicated content that can be made available in an acceptably short time-frame, and the related potential for storage of content. The use of CD ROMs or DVDs is one interim solution to a storage problem that is clearly going to disappear within a few years.

When asked, most training managers identify e-learning as the big technique they expect really to take off in the near future, but most also acknowledge that they are making very limited use of its potential at the moment. There may be a risk that clumsily put-together pilot initiatives will put off all but the most technologically literate managers, but most managers now use e-mail and Internet browsers so casually that they are likely to respond well to further development in this field.

The loneliness of the long-distance learner

As with distance learning, an element of self-reliance and personal discipline is required to overcome the lonelier aspect of using this technique, but e-learning offers greater potential to overcome this through contact with trainers and other managers who are learning. The use of chat rooms and online visual as well as aural contact should go some way to replicating the social climate of face-to-face learning situations, but can never hope to replace them completely.

While clearly suited to individual learning, the real potential for e-learning is in its use for group learning, not just in terms of economies of scale but perhaps more importantly in terms of improving the quality of the learning experience. Its interactivity means it can enable not just asynchronous learning but synchronous learning as well. It should suit all learning style preferences, and so no one should feel excluded.

E-learning is a further development from open and distance learning in the sense that it makes practical a step beyond modularization. It is now feasible to reduce elements of learning to the smallest possible units – learning objects or bytes – and construct programmes on a choice of any combination. Some people call this granularization, perhaps with tongue in cheek, but the serious point is that the technology enables the retention of innumerable learning objects in a repository or specialized database for easy retrieval as and when required.

The technology still represents something of an entry barrier to would-be new providers, especially small-scale ones, but size will be less of a barrier using online technology than it has been for new entrants in the old economy, since overheads are actually reduced. The technology barrier is more to do with understanding how to use it and keeping pace with new developments: as limitations vanish, the supply side of the market should mushroom.

Another cost advantage of e-learning is that publishing, and constantly revising and republishing, learning content becomes much cheaper as traditional print and production costs disappear. Distribution costs fall too, despite some initial capital outlay, as postage and packaging are all but eliminated. In addition, the use of online trainers at a distance represents a cost saving, as it does with traditional distance learning.

Web-based learning

The terms 'e-learning' and 'online learning' are sometimes used in a restricted sense, referring only to the most basic e-learning applications – essentially correspondence courses by e-mail. Web-based learning is then seen as a development from e-learning, offering managers (and others) the opportunity to utilize all the learning potential of the World Wide Web. Setting aside any debate over semantics, it is important to note that some of the most potent expressions of e-learning arise from the use of the Web.

At a time when many organizations speak of having corporate universities, and being – or becoming – learning organizations, it is the technology of the Web that makes these concepts possible and viable. Web-based systems can be used to store, manipulate and analyse phenomenal amounts of information about management development. And some applications do more.

Learning platforms

Perhaps the best-known Web-based learning platforms are Lotus Learning Space, Blackboard and Docent, but these are by no means the only options. Increasingly, forward-thinking business schools and other management development providers are rushing to offer the full range of their services online and to create cyberspace equivalents of their usual environments for management development.

Web-based learning is sometimes defined as involving the use of e-learning platforms to support online education. The leading Web sites offer: a means for trainers to run online programmes without confronting any of the technical obstacles; sophisticated record keeping made simple; and, for learning managers, the means to access not just tuition, but libraries, research facilities and online communities of learners.

More specialized Web sites concentrate on certain aspects only; for example, QuestionMark concentrates on providing customizable surveys, tests and assessment tools (see the section on assessment techniques later in the chapter).

Learning portals

Learning portals are a particular kind of Web site, and another valuable application. They are Web sites that go beyond the limitations of a single corporate site, offering information and access to a range of provision. Whether internal to a single organization or a collaboration among many, effectively these create virtual learning communities.

Virtual universities

Business schools and others that have set up their own systems offer virtual campus facilities where they attempt to simulate everything a learner would get from attending a university course, including not just the academic staples of coursework and library access, but virtual cafés or bars where the on-line students can meet informally and chat. It is too soon to judge what managers make of this technique, but it seems reasonable to assume it will appeal more to reflectors and theorists.

Virtual learning centres

See the section below on resource-based learning, and Case Study 13.

Case Study 11 – The growth curve of a new technique

The emergence and growth of e-learning as a new development technique has been unlike any other emergent new technique in living memory. As a general trend, e-business has reduced the incubation period for new business ideas, with the process from conception to business plan to commencement of trading reduced from many months (if not years) to just a few weeks. The business development process has been forced to keep up with the pace of technological change.

Similarly, e-learning has developed tools and systems faster than management development providers have been able to develop services making the most of them. The rise of e-learning has been meteoric in comparison with all previous techniques, and threatens to render some of them obsolete. An estimated 200 million people worldwide are using the Web, and that number is expected to double by 2003. This is the context in which organizations are investing more in e-learning than any other learning medium.

However, the initial emphasis has been on areas where a clear return can be seen on that investment, where mass participation takes place. Companies have concentrated so far on operational training needs, on induction, technical training and product knowledge, rather than on management development. This situation is likely to change rapidly and, by the time you read this, this characterization will be out of date. Thus far, we have many examples, but few exemplars, of management development by e-learning. Here are just a few:

- There are a growing number of university business schools offering online MBA programmes. Most of these are in the USA, although the City University of Hong Kong is a notable exception. A selection may be found at www.worldwidelearn.com/online-mba.htm.
- Other colleges and universities are forming consortia, partnering with publishers, e-commerce consultants, sales agents and others. Scottish Knowledge plc is one example, formed in 1997 with the support of 14 Scottish universities but since expanded to include 30 universities from the UK, USA and Australia, with offices in Washington, DC, Abu Dhabi and Kuala Lumpur. See www.scottish-knowledge.co.uk for further details.
- Publishers, especially electronic publishers, are extending their offers. McGraw-Hill Lifetime Learning is migrating its Xebec-branded CD ROMs to a new range of business skill modules by online learning. FT Dynamo, part of the Financial Times Group, is providing a suite of online resources including business news and information, journal articles and briefings, digests of latest thinking from business 'gurus', and a members' symposium featuring live conferencing.
- Business consultants are finding means to provide e-learning solutions. Ernst and Young have launched an e-learning venture, Intellinex, focusing on knowledge and online content development, offering 'everything from e-learning self-sufficiency to complete outsourcing support' (see www.intellinex.com).
- Companies are embarking on their own, in-house, e-learning initiatives. Motorola, for example, provide online management courses direct to the desktop (see Case Study 10 for more details).
- Learning resource centres are evolving into virtual versions (see, for example, Case Study 13).

The growth curve has reached the point of dramatic upturn – we can expect to see an explosion of management development by e-learning over the next few years.

Further reading

Parsloe, E and Barder, V (2001) *Making Electronic Learning Click*, Kogan Page, London

Rosenberg, M (2001) *e-learning*, McGraw-Hill, New York

Web references

www.blackboard.com
www.click2learn.com
www.docent.com
www.headlight.com
www.learn.com
www.learn2.com
www.learnitonline.com
www.LoginandLearn.com
www.lotus.com/home.nst/welcome/learningspace
www.smartforce.com
www.thinq.com

RESOURCE-BASED LEARNING

Group-work	
Individual	✔

One useful means of obtaining flexibility in off-the-job management development is by the use of a learning resource centre or by otherwise giving managers access to learning resources.

Private study and research

The oldest form of resource-based learning is private study, or detailed research into a topic of interest to a manager. This is often undertaken on the manager's own initiative and, as such, is perhaps not a management development technique, as the organization has not planned it. But it is possible to plan and direct this sort of activity – teachers do it all the time as the natural adjunct to coursework – and it is a powerful means of enabling managers to learn substantial amounts of theory.

Sometimes managers in a professional field will undertake advanced study for self-development, as for example when pursuing a doctorate or other qualification with professional standing. This will usually require the employer's support to be effective, and this yields an opportunity for the employer to shape or adapt the study experience to share in its benefits.

Guided reading

Guided reading programmes are a more proactive way of directing study, where the employer supplies books and organizes a reading programme with support for the manager undertaking the learning. This should mean more than simply handing over the reading matter. The 'guided' part means that the manager should be in regular consultation with his/her guide, discussing progress and reviewing the application of concepts in the reading to the manager's real work circumstances.

Of course, other reading material than books can also be provided. Most managers will do this on their own initiative, but employers can arrange for them to have subscriptions to newspapers, magazines or journals, or access to subscription-based electronic publications. Some organizations have libraries of relevant reading material.

An early form, which seems to have fallen out of fashion, was the reading circle or group, where a group of managers would meet on a regular basis. The meetings provided a motivational spur for managers to complete each phase of their reading, while the sessions themselves allowed for unclear concepts to be aired and clarified, and wider discussions to take place. Guided reading now seems to be regarded more as a one-to-one technique.

Computer-based training

Computer-based training, or CBT for short, is the technique by which training content is delivered to the learner on a desktop or laptop computer, perhaps stored on the computer's hard drive (in a training centre), or on floppy disks or CD ROMs if intended for use on the manager's PC. The term is falling out of favour as these forms of storage are superseded by Web-enabled technology, and CBT is sometimes included under the general heading of e-learning (see above).

However, CBT remains a useful means of providing management development, especially in generic people management skills, available in mass-published training products. There remains the question of whether to provide the training at the manager's desktop or within a specially set-up learning resource centre.

Learning resource centres

These are also known as learning centres, or open learning centres, and sometimes given names unique to the host organization (see, for example, Case Study 12). The essence of this technique is to provide facilities to make a range of learning resources available for borrowing, or on-site use in a corporate centre (or centres).

Resources other than books are typically designed for use in a distance learning programme, including self-study workbooks and packs, audiotapes, floppy disks and to some extent video-tapes. The significant exception is CD ROMs, which have more usually been designed to be deployed on stand-alone PCs in an organization's learning resource centre.

However, all of these resources may be held in a library – or resource centre – and made available to managers for self-learning, and this is now common practice in many major corporations. The benefit of flexibility is obvious. Many organizations also use their centre as a means of encouraging greater uptake of learning and promoting a learning organization. The downside is the lack of personal (ie human) support inherent in the resources.

Unlike traditional libraries complementing traditional courses, learning resource centres offer flexible back-up to whatever forms of development managers are engaged in. For example, managers on a competence programme can access support materials as and when they need them.

Pros and cons

There may be significant set-up costs for a new learning resource centre, in terms of both capital outlay and an initial stock of consumable resources. These may be defrayed by parallel reduc-tion of alternative provision, such as day-release courses, but the value of the expenditure should be measured in terms of centre use and measurable outcomes at work. Most organizations with established centres cannot imagine how they ever managed without one.

Reflectors and theorists will like this technique, but pragmatists and activists are likely to find it more limiting. Also, some organi-zations have found that managers tend to use the centre less than other employees. This may be due to the corporate culture, or the nature of the resources held in the centre, but there should be no problem here that cannot be overcome by marketing the centre in the right way: specialist visiting sessions restricted to managers only may help stimulate greater uptake.

There is a view that e-learning represents a threat to this tech-nique and may make it redundant. This assumes that the provision of online learning to the desktop will circumvent dedicated centres. But one of the arguments in favour of the learning resource centre is that it offers a distraction-free environment, as opposed to the interruptions and disturbances managers may have at their desks (particularly in open-plan offices). This argument still holds in the context of e-learning, suggesting the nature and location of the resources may change but the centre will still be in demand.

The virtual learning centre

Some organizations are now moving towards virtual learning centres, which may ultimately lead to the disappearance of the physical centre. These are rather like limited versions of virtual universities (see above) except that their model is the learning resource centre. A manager travelling, or staying away from home or the office, is able to access the centre online via a laptop and a telephone line, select appropriate resources and either study them online or download them to study later.

Case Study 12 – Standard Life

The Standard Life Assurance Company is the largest mutual society in Europe, and a giant of the financial services industry. It has a 'Triple A' rating for financial strength from Standard & Poor's, as it has over £75 billion in funds under management, which is equivalent to the combined values of Marks and Spencer, Tesco, Boots, Cadbury Schweppes and British Airways. Standard Life employs around 9,000 staff (excluding operations outside the UK), 7,000 of which are based in the company's home city of Edinburgh.

Open access development centre

In 1996, Standard Life set up its first open access development centre (OADC) to provide staff and management with an alternative way to learn from traditional training courses and to help the company develop personal competences for all. Since then, a further six centres have been opened, in each of the company's main buildings in Edinburgh. The centres are equipped with standard multimedia PCs, audio and video equipment, soft furnishings, personal study booths and training or meeting rooms of varying sizes.

The centres hold a library of about 1,500 different resources, of which around 800 are books, 300 videos, 300 computer-based training packages (mainly CD ROMs) and 100 audiotape programmes. Managers and staff can find out what resources are available by visiting a centre, consulting a member of OADC staff or via the company's intranet. The OADC staff book the resources required and make sure they are available when the manager arrives, show him/her how to use the package and make sure s/he is comfortable. For managers unable to come into one of the Edinburgh centres, a lending library service is available whereby resources are mailed out. Remote managers can use the multimedia resources on their office computers or in some cases their laptops.

OADC staff run the centres, provide the library service, offer general development advice, and help with advice and administration of individual learning accounts.

Resources

The resources held in the OADCs cover a wide range of subject matter including product knowledge on life assurance and pensions, and materials that generally meet operational development needs, the full extent of management development topics and general business knowledge, IT skills and anything relevant to the attainment of Standard Life's personal competences. They link into a number of company-wide initiatives, including the competence framework, a total customer satisfaction programme and a contribution management process.

In 2000, the centres were used 22,000 times by 4,500 different members of staff (ie about half of the total headcount). These figures include only the core of actual visits to an OADC involving booking a study booth, to which must be added a large number of library loans and other services uses. These usage levels provide the essential justification for the OADCs, on the basis that if managers and staff use them they must value them. This is supplemented by the gathering of anecdotal evidence to support reports. Andy Tucker, Standard Life's Learning Technologies Manager, believes the OADCs are a success because of the learning culture within Standard Life, but acknowledges that this is a circular argument, as the centres actually help develop and maintain that culture.

There are plans to continue to build and develop the OADC service. This will mean not just more of the same, but also making an increasing number of services available direct to the desktop, demonstrating that there is no contradiction between having dedicated learning resource centres and providing resource-based learning in other ways.

Case Study 13 – Ashridge VLRC

Ashridge, the international business school based in Berkhamsted, Hertfordshire, just outside London, traces its origins back to the foundation of a Benedictine monastery on the site in 1283. It was established as a charitable trust by Act of Parliament in 1954, and since 1959 has concentrated exclusively on management education. Ashridge has been involved in electronic publishing and learning developments for the last six years, and in 1998 launched its Virtual Learning Resource Centre (VLRC).

Going virtual

Ashridge already had a 'traditional' learning resource centre, but three significant business changes prompted the virtual development. Its business was becoming more international, rather than mainly UK-based; clients' courses were getting shorter and shorter; and long courses like the MBA were becoming more modular. All of this suggested the need for a more flexible service, and the VLRC is now used by a variety of corporate clients worldwide, including Xerox Europe, Volkswagen, and WM Mercer, especially its New York offices. Through the involvement of the Foreign and Commonwealth Office, the VLRC may be accessed at any British embassy in the world.

The resources are available to Ashridge staff and alumni, current MBA and other course students, and managers from corporate clients by subscription. The VLRC offers remote access, from home, work or when travelling, to a vast array of resources, and a global network for contacts with other users through online discussion forums.

The resources include around 50 learning guides on skills, competences and techniques in management, written by Ashridge faculty members. Each guide contains a 10- to 12-page overview of leading thinking, recommended resources for further development, and practical development activities. Examples of the subjects covered by the learning guides include brand management, costing and management accounting, e-business, investment appraisal, lifestyle planning, supply chain management, writing a business plan and many more. Among the other resources are reviews of recently published books and training resources, a bookshop catalogue with links to amazon.com, economic overviews and country forecasts, articles from Ashridge's *Directions* journal, and software guides based on the 'ski run' principle (blue for beginners, red for the more familiar and black for advanced users). In addition, subscribers get access via live links to Web-based general reference information and databases.

Technological infrastructure

Organizations subscribe in one of three ways. The VLRC was developed in industry-standard Web-based software, so can be copied via CD ROM on to a corporate intranet, or by replication with the Ashridge server for intranet servers that run on Lotus Domino, or can be accessed via the Internet at www.ashridge.org/virtual. Some organizations elect to use a combination of these options, without incurring any financial penalty.

Managers use the VLRC between study modules on Master's programmes, or for just-in-time learning, or, in Ashridge's most successful applications, in integration with other management development initiatives such as appraisals or personal development plans (as, for example, with the District Audit organization). Often the learning guides are linked into company-specific competence frameworks and then incorporated into the company's intranet using the language and conventions recognized within that company.

Evaluating success

The concept is described by Andrew Ettinger, Ashridge's Director of Learning Resources, as 'an integration of learning and information, bringing together knowledge management and e-learning in a single application'. Looking ahead to the next innovation, Ettinger is developing the VLRC to provide 'learning bytes' – short, sharp inputs of around 20–40 minutes' duration each. Both now and in the future, the Virtual Learning Resource Centre offers access to all the resources Ashridge can bring together, 'at a click'.

Corporate clients also value the use of this resource as a management development technique. Deutsche Bank users appreciate the way learning is allowed to happen on the job alongside all sorts of other activities. Scottish Power managers see it as the cornerstone of an online business school.

Further reading

Brown, S and Smith, B (1996) *Resource-Based Learning*, Kogan Page, London

Web references

www.goodpractice.net
www.inst-mgt.org.uk/micweb/explorer/micweb4.htm
www.netg.com
www.trainingsupersite.com

ASSESSMENT TECHNIQUES

Group-work	
Individual	✔

The variety of assessment techniques that are usually deployed chiefly to test what learning has been accomplished can also be used as learning techniques in their own right. Everyone has experienced the impending test (even if it was only at school) and the impetus it provided to cram – but learning comes not only from the preparation but also from the test itself. Following this logic, open learning workbooks, computer-based packages and online learning programmes use periodic 'self-tests', often at the end of a section, to help managers review their learning.

Formative and summative assessment

When an assessment technique is used to help a trainer and a learner to measure their progress, this is known as formative assessment. This distinguishes it from summative assessment, which is used at the end of a learning experience to test achievement. The same techniques may be used for either purpose. When one of the goals of learning is assessment for a qualification, the formative assessment helps prepare the learners, while the summative assessment is what determines whether they actually get the qualification.

Assessment on a course – and sometimes other forms of development – is usually with a view to the attainment of some sort of qualification. But for trainers, the point of assessment is more usually for directly work-related objectives: to determine whether learners are ready to take on new work, how well they are doing with work in progress or whether they are ready to take a new career step.

Thus managers can learn, and management development providers can plan to help them learn, by the use of an array of techniques like:

- essays;
- reports;
- multiple-choice tests;
- examinations.

Competence-based assessment is a specialist field, with different assessment instruments emerging as more common than conventional ones, especially the use of portfolios (see Case Study 26).

In many instances, trainers will have to write their own assessment instruments, although awarding bodies usually set their own exams and so forth, but some companies provide this service and many are now springing up online. Costs are not high: the most expensive assessment is one that has been written by an in-house trainer over a number of days. And costs per learner, for repeated use of the same instruments, yield rapid economies of scale.

We all know that some people like exams and some don't. Most assessment techniques are of a similar design and favour reflectors and pragmatists. The portfolio of evidence of competence is perhaps an exception, and certainly appeals to a different type of person: activists may prefer portfolios.

Case Study 14 – The Scottish Qualifications Authority

The Scottish education system has been described as the envy of the world, and nurses a reputation dating back over at least two centuries, during which it has cradled talents of world renown, which have generated many of the inventions and discoveries we take for granted today.

A single assessment body

In the 1980s, Scottish vocational education pioneered some approaches and techniques that have since become commonplace around the world. The body that led these was the Scottish Vocational Education Council, which has since become part of the unitary Scottish Qualifications Authority (SQA). This is now the single body that accredits and awards all qualifications in Scotland, whether academic or vocational, and whether through schools, colleges or independent training providers.

One defining characteristic of Scottish qualifications is that they are typically modular – capable of being achieved by increments. Another is that their specific assessment is capable of being tailored to meet the actual circumstances of the manager – or other candidate – preparing for assessment.

Ensuring consistency

SQA sets annual examinations in many disciplines, but also provides assessment criteria – but not instruments – in many more. SQA assessment criteria determine how a manager undertaking a college course has coursework marked. Whether for a full-time Higher National Certificate in Management, a Scottish Vocational Qualification in Management or a modular programme leading to a Unit Award in just one aspect of management, there will be consistent national rules set by the SQA on how the college assesses the manager. The college retains the devolved authority to carry out assessments, but must meet strict quality controls and operate within the criteria laid down by the SQA. This provides a system with validity, reliability and practicability.

For example, in order to be awarded a Higher National Certificate, a candidate has to achieve the number of unit credits prescribed by the SQA. Within each unit, s/he has to be assessed against performance criteria laid down by the SQA to demonstrate attainment of the appropriate standard in each case. But the college or centre will carry out the actual assessments, using whatever instruments it chooses, in the times and places it chooses.

The SQA defines assessment as measuring the evidence of a candidate's attainment of knowledge, understanding and skills against defined criteria. Through validation and centre approval procedures, external monitoring and quality assurance, it seeks to devolve that assessment as close as possible to the learner, in the belief that this means more accurate assessment.

Against this background, the SQA defines a range of assessment techniques, including:

- written examinations or tests (question papers);
- projects or coursework (including investigations, assignments, dissertations and case studies);
- oral assessments;
- tests and observations of performance;
- skill demonstrations.

In addition, the SQA defines a range of ways of authenticating candidates' work in cases of indirect assessment where observation is not possible, including:

- questioning;
- use of personal logs;
- personal statements by candidates;
- peer reports;
- witness testimony;
- write-ups under supervised conditions;
- countersigning of work.

These arrangements are not unique, and similar provision is made in many countries throughout the world, sometimes based on quite different belief systems and performance standards. The SQA model is an exemplar, but by no means the only one. Time will tell whether it produces such results – and such people – as have emerged in the last 200 years.

Further reading

Fletcher, S (2000) *Competence-Based Assessment Techniques*, Kogan Page, London

Scottish Qualifications Authority (1999) *Guide to Assessment and Quality Assurance*, SQA, Glasgow

Web references

www.questionmark.com
www.web4test.com

DEVELOPMENT CENTRES

Group-work	✔
Individual	

These are sometimes also known as developmental assessment centres or management development centres.

Development centres are concentrated multi-activity events, usually held within a single organization, taking place over two or three days (or sometimes longer). They are a development from assessment centres, which are similar events used mainly for recruitment and selection. Development centres are meant to de-emphasize the assessment aspect, although it often remains crucial since the purpose of an organization holding a development centre is frequently to gauge potential and help make selections for promotion (or similar). Instead they are intended to focus on opportunities for personal development and as such are more akin to courses than to selection interviews.

By definition, they take place off the job, comprising attendance at an in-company event that may include any or all of the following components:

- group-work;
- counselling;
- interviews;
- discussions;
- exercises;
- activities;
- psychometric assessments.

Development centres can be key tools for management development, as they are a direct means of addressing strategic issues for an organization, such as employee resourcing, career and succession planning. And they provide enough variety to appeal to all types of learning style preference.

History

They are a relatively recent phenomenon: management development texts of the 1970s and 80s never mention development
centres and rarely mention assessment centres. Although some
claim the latter date back to 1942, their use seems to have been
restricted to the military for many years. More recently, online
technology has begun to change development centres, as information such as responses to questionnaires can be gathered remotely
prior to the event. This means the event itself can be shorter and
perhaps more meaningful given the prior knowledge gained by
the organizers.

Costs

They tend to be expensive. The skills of running a successful centre
take a long time to learn, and it takes a lot of people to run a centre
– interviewers, facilitators, observers and others. While centres
don't need to be designed from scratch every time, and some
providers have off-the-shelf offerings that require only minimal
tailoring, they still cost a lot of money – perhaps 10 times as much
as a short course of equal length. This means they are used far
more by organizations that have the scale to think big with
budgets, but significantly these organizations tend to stick with
them, suggesting they provide good value for money.

Case Study 15 – Otis

Otis Limited installs and maintains passenger and freight elevators, escala-
tors and travelators, and is part of the aerospace and building systems
conglomerate United Technologies Corporation, based in Connecticut,
USA. The Otis name is synonymous with lifts, dating back to origins in
New York in 1853. Its UK and Ireland business turns over £240 million
and employs 2,700 people.

In 1996, Otis wanted to diagnose skill needs and improve the performance of 24 senior managers, towards a strategic objective of continu-
ously improving customer satisfaction. They decided to buy in the support
of a firm of external consultants to take advantage of off-the-shelf exercises
and specialist inputs, and chose Saville and Holdsworth Limited (SHL).

Using job analysis

Working closely with Otis's Commercial Operations Director and his team, SHL designed a development centre, drawing upon their general experience and the specific circumstances of their client. They used job analysis techniques together with a standard SHL instrument, the Perspectives in Management Competencies Inventory, to establish priorities for the competences against which managers were to be assessed and developed. The competences fell into the following domains: managerial, professional, entrepreneurial and personal qualities.

Making the centre work

The development centre itself included a diverse range of activities: the Occupational Personality Questionnaire, a high-level ability test, an in-tray exercise, observed interactive exercises, structured interviews and a final feedback interview.

Thus Otis and SHL ensured that the centre afforded managers the chance to demonstrate all of the key competence areas, and opportunities for focused individual feedback immediately afterwards. The feedback provided the basis for the formation of individual action plans for development against the competences.

Normal SHL practice is to train the next tier of senior managers in the client company to act as observers and assessors during the centre exercises. In this case, it was not possible, as the most senior managers in the company were participants themselves – therefore SHL consultants fulfilled these roles.

Outcomes

The outcomes of the development centre included:

- powerful, detailed information for the company on the competence of its senior management team;
- increased self-awareness for participating managers;
- developmental action plans for each senior manager;
- specific modular training programmes in critical competence areas.

Further reading

Woodruffe, C (2000) *Development and Assessment Centres: Identifying and assessing competence*, CIPD, London

6

On-the-job techniques

This chapter deals with those techniques that take place predominantly on the job or in 'real time'. It may be argued that any pause to develop a manager – however short that pause may be – means attention is removed from the work being undertaken. In this sense, all management techniques are off the job. However, this book maintains the distinction, which is widely understood, between on-the-job and off-the-job techniques.

Initially, it may seem surprising that the majority of on-the-job techniques are for use with a single learner. On reflection, it makes sense that these techniques, which seek not to interfere with work in progress, will tend to avoid bringing learners together (as this would take at least one away from his/her work).

This range of techniques includes those that are best suited to competence development. It is logical that an approach that seeks to improve managers' capability to perform tasks or functions should be best served by techniques that not only take place at work but seek to exploit what managers actually do, to further their development.

This chapter deals with:

- sitting by Nellie;
- instruction;

- secondment;
- coaching and related techniques;
- team building;
- action learning;
- work-based projects;
- performance and development review;
- forms of learning record;
- discovery learning.

Three of these techniques – sitting by Nellie, instruction (including demonstration) and discovery learning – are elementary techniques common in other forms of employee development but of limited usefulness in management development. Accordingly, our treatment of these is more restricted than that of the other techniques in this chapter.

SITTING BY NELLIE

Group-work	
Individual	✔

The most obvious form of on-the-job development is that of working alongside an experienced practitioner in order to observe and copy his/her good practice. This is universally known as 'sitting by Nellie'. Operator and craft skills have traditionally been taught primarily by this method, cerebral skills (such as are required in management) less so. The weakness of the method is that the learner can only ever be as good as 'Nellie', who may not always be the best role model. Its enduring strength is that it is simple to implement and low in visible oncosts.

With managers, the method is more likely to be described as 'shadowing' or similar. It will carry the explicit aim of observing and learning from how the experienced manager handles specific obligations or situations, rather than encouraging the learning manager to copy his/her role model's overall behaviour. Clearly there are limitations to what can be achieved for management development by this technique, even if the learning manager is able constantly to question the role model as to why s/he acts as s/he does.

Encouraging women

Shadowing, or role modelling, is an increasingly common technique for developing and promoting women managers. Many initiatives, in many countries, aim to combat ingrained sex discrimination and the 'glass ceiling' on women's careers by matching promising women managers with more experienced role models, as Case Study 16 illustrates. At this point, the distinction becomes blurred between this technique and some of those in the coaching cluster, notably mentoring and sponsoring (see later in the chapter).

The cheap assistant

One variant on shadowing, which is popular in some companies, is for inexperienced managers to be assigned to 'executive assistant' roles, where they work with experienced and senior managers to obtain an appreciation of the scope of their roles. The lead motivation for this approach is usually not management development but the desire of senior managers to obtain the service of bright young assistants.

Deputizing

Another variant occurs when a manager is designated as the deputy for another, usually more senior, manager, and 'stands in' for him/her when s/he is unavailable. When this takes place over a sustained period, it is sometimes called 'acting up'. If the deputy is prepared in advance, then this is a good extension of the sitting-by-Nellie model, an opportunity to practise what has been studied; if not, then it is just another form of discovery learning (see later in the chapter).

Pros and cons

The biggest perceived advantage of this technique is cost: because there is no oncost, the assumption is that it is inexpensive. Of course, this ignores the cost in time to both the 'Nellie' and the apprentice, and the opportunity cost of whatever else Nellie doesn't do. Yet clearly it is a relatively inexpensive technique.

It is also difficult for anyone to object to getting involved in this sort of development, although theorists in particular may find it frustrating. But these are negative reasons: while there must be a place for this technique, it should only be in the context of being combined with other, more stimulating, methods.

Many organizations strive to inculcate a positive attitude among all their managers (and other staff) to this kind of learning transfer. There is a widespread feeling that it helps to have everyone think in terms of all work contacts holding out the possibility of sharing information, passing on knowledge and understanding, and facilitating learning. In this view, good practice like 'sitting by Nellie' is the cornerstone of a learning organization. You do not have to go all the way down the road to accepting this view to see that it offers a potentially useful perspective for management and organizational development.

Case Study 16 – Network Ireland

Network Ireland is an organization founded in 1983 to promote the role of women in business and encourage women to develop in their careers as managers. It is based on individual membership and currently has over 1,000 members, comprising women in managerial roles from a variety of backgrounds, including those working in government bodies, major multinational companies, the professions and the arts, and owner-managers of small firms, throughout the Republic of Ireland. It is supported by Bank of Ireland Business Banking.

The very existence of the organization means that there is an informal network through which women benefit from one another's experiences. But Network Ireland does much more: it facilitates a number of formal programmes of shadowing, mentoring and role modelling, which provide not just figureheads to emulate but support structures to ensure benefits are gained and can be measured.

Careful consideration is given to the selection of role models, who are drawn from a panel of management experts with experience in business counselling, sourced through a variety of commercial organizations. All role models are referred and recommended by their peers, and subject to confidentiality agreements.

There is a matching process, whereby managers and role models are linked against the criteria of specific business disciplines needed, location, industry sector and (after initial meetings) personal fit. The boundaries of the relationship are clearly defined: the role models may provide advice but not actually carry out tasks on behalf of the managers – they cannot function as professional consultants.

What happens after that will depend upon the individuals involved. There may be time spent in the role model's environment, shadowing her activities; there may be time spent in the manager's environment, looking over her shoulder; there will certainly be off-the-job meetings. What is important is that there is real contact, sharing of work time, and the opportunity for the managers to learn from the role models' experience and example.

Network Ireland find that this system works well. Its members are happy with the service, and active development is taking place, affording women opportunities that would not otherwise be available.

Further reading

Rainbird, H (ed) (2000) *Training in the Workplace*, Macmillan, London
Rylatt, A (2001) *Learning Unlimited*, Kogan Page, London

INSTRUCTION

Group-work	
Individual	✔

This is the simplest and perhaps most obvious – even banal – way of developing a manager.

On-the-job instruction occurs when the learner does not merely 'sit by Nellie' but is explicitly directed by her (or him). A series of orders or instructions is issued in a planned attempt to direct the learner's behaviour. This encompasses everything from the random individual instructions given as the natural adjunct of the 'sitting-by-Nellie' approach to a planned programme of instruction designed to cover a range of aspects in a job role. Although more common in operator or craft training, this technique may be applied in a limited way to the development of managers.

The obvious applications of this technique are in teaching managers to follow set procedures or to complete administrative paperwork correctly. It is less likely, for practical reasons, that the technique will be appropriate to teaching managers how to manage operations overall or, even more so, how to manage people. Arguably, this is more about training than development, but it may be particularly helpful in developing competence.

Instructions may be set down in writing rather than just delivered verbally; they may be supported by the use of checklists or by the use of some kind of script or schedule. Here the technique begins to blur with programmed learning, or the issuing of handouts to support coursework.

Demonstration

In practical, skill-based disciplines, the addition of the concept of demonstration would be obvious and, for trainers, axiomatic. Its use is less obvious in management development, but it is the logical follow-on from instruction. The principle is that the trainer instructs, then demonstrates and then gives the manager the opportunity to practise the skill. The cliché that 'actions speak louder than words' summarizes the thinking behind it – as managers see what they are to learn as well as being told about it, and then are encouraged to try things for themselves.

Demonstration using a surrogate environment can be a useful variation, albeit an off-the-job one. The use of samba drumming to demonstrate a style of leadership was highlighted in Case Study 3. Another recent example was Manchester Business School's use of horse-whispering to demonstrate less aggressive management styles. Creative management development professionals may be able to find unlikely analogies like these on the job too.

There is a danger of instruction being overlooked in the development of managers, but this technique has its place, albeit perhaps for the more mundane aspects of management and, like everything else, it helps provide variety. It will probably appeal most to activists, but all managers will expect to receive instruction throughout their careers, and may benefit from it even if they are unaware that the intention is developmental.

Case Study 17 – Krib Naidoo

Krib Naidoo is Commercial Manager with a contract manufacturing company in Malaysia. The company makes electronic components to order for major international branded goods. Krib's role is to liaise with the brand-holders, identify business opportunities, help secure manufacturing contracts and ensure contract compliance. It is a highly competitive industry with many alternative manufacturing facilities available, low pricing and tight margins.

Receiving instruction

When Krib joined the company, he had to undergo an extensive induction process, which consisted mainly of sessions with a variety of specialists in various functions, each explaining how they needed him to follow certain procedures. The Purchasing Manager went through the forms to fill out to ensure supply of raw materials in good time for each contract; the Finance Manager covered the accounting procedures for each job; the Human Resource Manager went through the system for employee resourcing and the Commercial Manager's role in identifying forward staffing needs; the Production Manager covered the notification procedure for bringing a new order on line; and there were others. All of them used the same approach of putting the paperwork on the desk in front of them and then going over it line by line.

Krib found this very boring. His background in sales and customer service meant he enjoyed interaction with people, the cut and thrust of negotiating, and some of the more creative aspects of his job. He knew he had to get the details right and put in the time to complete the administration, but he found it hard to concentrate on the initially overwhelming volume of procedural information. In his first year, as he brought his first contracts in, he made many procedural mistakes, none of them particularly costly, but enough to cause inconvenience and incur the displeasure of his senior colleagues.

Refreshing the instruction

Towards the end of his first year, Krib asked each of the managers who had contributed to his induction to repeat their instructions. They got out the forms and followed the same process as before, instructing Krib on how to fill in each section. Krib found this much more helpful than the first time, as he now had a fair idea of what was expected, the paperwork was more familiar and he felt under less pressure. He asked more questions and developed a deeper understanding of both what he had to do and, crucially, why.

Krib knew the second instruction sessions, a year down the line, had been more beneficial than the first, but he also knew the information was needed before then. This seemed an irreconcilable conflict, until he observed what happened on the production lines when a job was in progress. There were laminated cards at each workstation, and copies bound into a manual in each work area, setting out the procedures to be followed. Thus, whenever employees were unsure what to do, they checked the written instruction first.

The conclusion seemed obvious – write down a similar set of procedures for the role of the Commercial Manager. But it hasn't happened yet. Krib is the only Commercial Manager in the company, and he doesn't need the written instructions any more. Krib thinks he would like to write them up himself before he moves on to his next job – if he ever gets the time. He knows that if he doesn't, his successor will go through the same series of instruction sessions as he did.

SECONDMENT

Group-work	
Individual	✔

This is also known, in certain contexts, as an attachment, a job swap, a job rotation or a transfer.

Sometimes a manager can derive great benefit from being 'seconded' for a limited period of time to a new role, perhaps managing a different function, more likely performing a role similar to his/her substantive role but in a different location or context. Such secondments are common within large companies or groups of companies, but may also occur with secondment to an external organization, often a charity or community organization.

Companies implement this technique to broaden the horizons of the learning manager, exposing him/her to new situations and giving him/her new perspectives. Where a reciprocal secondment takes place, this is sometimes called an exchange, a 'job swap' or, by those who favour the language of sport, a 'transfer'.

One common form of secondment is when a manager is sent abroad, since an assignment to another country, even to what is ostensibly the same role, can offer significant learning opportunities. Large organizations may do this partly as a means of ensuring consistent staffing levels in less attractive locations, or to encourage the global mobility of their workforce. Some industry organizations, such as chambers of commerce, specialize in providing overseas secondments to managers from smaller firms that lack the international scale to follow the large organizations' example.

Many organizations find that it is much better for a good understanding of the detailed workings and key challenges facing different functional areas and business units that managers have actually worked in these areas. As a consequence, many take a structured approach to divisional or departmental exchanges and arrange for managers to follow a set programme of secondments as part of their induction or as a core element of their graduate or new manager development programmes. This is sometimes termed 'job rotation'.

Job rotation

Job rotation could perhaps be seen as a variant on secondment, as it usually involves a manager moving from one role to another or being 'rotated' through a range of available managerial roles. Graduate development programmes may deploy this technique to introduce learning managers to the range of requirements and opportunities within the organization, prior to deciding where to place each manager on a more permanent basis. Some would differentiate this technique from secondment by the criterion that secondment usually involves returning to the substantive role, whereas job rotation usually does not.

Various other exchange or placement programmes are operated for which their advocates would claim significant differences from secondment and job rotation. Here are five possibilities:

- accepting a position of responsibility within a charitable or voluntary organization on a part-time or voluntary basis (ie while continuing in the substantive role);
- attachment to a customer's organization as a representative;
- assignment to a government committee, agency or quango;
- assignment to a company or industry committee;
- attachment to a manager with strong development skills.

The only criterion by which these would seem to warrant separate classification is that they need not be full-time commitments, but all of them retain the same basic characteristic or developmental motive of seeking to place the manager in a new situation for a limited time. One of these 'attachments' – to a manager with 'strong development skills' – anticipates the next set of techniques (coaching etc).

Pros and cons

Secondments should appeal most to activists, although beyond the immediate term the experience should yield opportunities of interest to all types of learning style preference. They are bound to have great appeal for many managers, notably the more adventurous spirits, but may cause problems by leaving gaps in the managers' substantive roles and consonant disruption to normal working practices.

The costs of secondments will vary greatly: usually they will appear to cost little or nothing, but costs can be particularly high in those cases where the employer seconds managers but continues to meet their salaries and other employment costs.

Case Study 18 – Bob Gunning

Bob Gunning is a banker by profession and has been since he joined the former National Commercial Bank of Scotland as a trainee in 1968. Most of his career has been spent with the Royal Bank of Scotland.

The Royal Bank of Scotland Group is one of the UK's largest banks and has been one of the top 20 listed companies in the UK since its acquisition in 2000 of the National Westminster Bank. Its other subsidiaries include Direct Line, Citizens Financial Group and Ulster Bank. It employs around 94,000 people and retains its group headquarters in Edinburgh, where it was founded in 1727.

The banking industry has changed beyond all recognition during Bob Gunning's career, which (so far) has spanned more than three decades. After 10 years in traditional banking occupations, Bob moved into management in 1978 and filled a variety of positions, rising to Regional Manager for central Scotland by 1991.

Project Columbus

In 1992, the bank embarked upon a major re-engineering project, code-named 'Columbus', and much to his surprise Bob was approached to undertake a secondment to the project: his role was Leader of the Personal Sector Strategy Team. Thus began a three-and-a-half-year secondment that Bob still describes as the most significant work of his career.

Columbus involved more than 100 people in a multi-disciplinary project team, aiming to rebuild the bank totally and become a world-class organization. The process was facilitated by McKinsey consultants, but on the basis that they would show the bank's managers how to analyse and re-engineer their business (rather than just doing it for them) and give them the ability to do to others what they had done to themselves. Bob believes this was a key factor in the successful integration with NatWest. Almost incidentally to its main purpose, the project had a huge developmental impact on the team members, shaking up their perceptions of the world of banking and their roles within it.

What Bob did

Bob Gunning's role was to manage a team of 10 people in an environment liberated from the bank's usual structures – there were no staff grades, no business cards, and open-plan offices. Bob admits he found the process at first discomfiting, often having to ask people to undertake work he was unfamiliar with himself, and with tensions when people couldn't see the value of the work they were to do or resented undertaking tasks they would normally have delegated to their subordinates.

At the initial business analysis phase he felt out of his depth, but this changed as the project moved on to the implementation phase, as he was much more comfortable with making things happen. McKinsey consultants helped him write a work plan for his team, he became a more effective team leader and he learnt how to do business analysis. The project's two-monthly reporting cycle meant he got used to the discipline of making regular presentations to the bank's senior executive.

Perhaps Bob's most significant contribution to the re-engineering was to lead the team that designed and implemented the prototype 'new bank', initially in Glasgow, and then Edinburgh and the rest of Scotland. There was a lot of work around shaping the new job roles, selecting people to fill them through targeted selection procedures and competence-based interviews, and then implementing the new system.

What Bob did next

At the end of all this, Bob applied for, and was selected for, one of the new roles he'd helped design, as Director of Commercial Banking for the east of Scotland, effectively head of the bank's sales force dealing with corporate customers in the £1 million to £5 million turnover range. Effectively, the secondment had been the vehicle for him to move on into an enhanced role within the bank.

The secondment taught him the value of business projects, to the extent that some of his colleagues say he's now more interested in projects than people (a charge he denies). A recent successful example has been the creation of an investment fund for the east of Scotland, with hard-won European Union support. He has learnt to persevere in finding ways around obstacles, and his watchword is now 'making things happen'.

Further reading

Chater, S and Stokes, H (1992) *Sharing Skills: Making the most of secondments,* CRAC, Cambridge

COACHING AND RELATED TECHNIQUES

Group-work	
Individual	✔

There are a number of techniques that, taken together, may be viewed as the provision of flexible, relatively informal support on a one-to-one basis, often by a more experienced senior colleague or sometimes a specialist who may come from outside the organization. All of these techniques can include formal interview sessions, which naturally take place off the job, but for all of them the focus is on the job – the best coaching, for example, occurs casually in the workplace.

Some prefer to talk sweepingly of coaching as a generic label for all of the techniques in this section, but it is more accurate to think of them as a cluster, consisting of five distinct types:

- coaching;
- counselling;
- mentoring;
- networking;
- sponsoring.

Some management development professionals distinguish these techniques as being either 'catalytic' or 'reactive', arguing that the one is simply about the trainer helping the manager to change, while the other is about both participants changing together. It doesn't really matter which category each fits in, for our purposes: in either case, the manager is helped to change. However, this does raise an interesting point about the developmental potential of being the coach – see the section on discovery learning at the end of this chapter.

Coaching versus counselling and mentoring

To begin with the core technique of the cluster, coaching is about enabling learners with tasks and directing them with functions; it is fundamentally task- or function-focused, and is concerned with improving skills, competence and performance. This distinguishes it from counselling, which is about helping people with personal concerns such as motivation and self-confidence. It also helps distinguish it from mentoring, which goes beyond tasks or functions and looks at capability, potential and career-related personal development.

Coaching is sometimes further explained by distinguishing it from one-to-one coursework or instruction (see earlier in the chapter) via the distinction that teaching and instruction direct someone to exactly what they are to do, whereas coaching helps them work it out for themselves. Coaching is thus seen as more valuable in helping managers learn or empowering them.

Some management development professionals revere mentoring and elevate it to the status of the most valuable technique, describing it as one of the most powerful developmental approaches there are. In this vision, the mentor is the consigliere to the mafia godfather, the manager. Mentoring certainly embraces a range of activities, from positive role modelling to advising to future gazing, but a less enthusiastic observer might see it as merely advanced coaching.

Certainly in practice the distinctions are often blurred. Indeed, many of the most sophisticated examples of coaching programmes that can be recognized and described in any detail have tended to involve predominantly formal off-the-job sessions. This does not diminish the on-the-job impact, as the following case study shows.

Case Study 19 – Consignia

Consignia, formerly the Post Office Group, is a public corporation owned, but not managed, by the British Government, providing a wide range of business and consumer mail and related services throughout the UK and beyond. It embraces three well-known brands, the Post Office Network, Royal Mail and Parcelforce, which are operated by 19 customer-facing profit centres or business units. The organization employs nearly 200,000 people, of which 30,000 are managers, from first-line supervisors to managing director level. Further information is available on www.postoffice.co.uk.

Competitive pressures

In the late 1990s, Consignia faced three challenges: international competition was growing, especially with competitors like the Dutch and the Germans being less restricted by government legislation, which meant its competitiveness was weakened; new technologies, such as mobile phones and e-mail, were increasingly providing substitutes for traditional postal services, so its market share was falling; and regulatory pressures, notably from the European Commission, were threatening to open up still further the market for domestic mail, favouring private sector competitors.

Senior management at Consignia recognized that if the business was to survive it needed to add more value than just to provide a series of commodity products. Such customization required much more from the individual in terms of added value. This required a new management style and a new type of manager in what was overwhelmingly a people business – its old culture of 'command and control' would not be appropriate to its new circumstances and there was a need to encourage individual initiative within a strict service framework. This was seen as best achieved by a move to an environment where coaching was a key element of the relationship between supervisor and supervised, and the concept of 'leaders as coaches' emerged. Experiences of coaching for individual managers had provided some evidence that this was both possible and desirable. One senior manager was very capable in his executive role, but his effectiveness at board level was widely doubted: after support from an external coach, he was able to take on the managing director position with one of the business units, and to play an effective role on the board of the Post Office Network.

Stimulating organizational change

Success stories like this convinced senior management of the need for a comprehensive coaching programme, which they began to implement from 1998. Led by the then Director of Personnel, Graham Cater, they invested around £0.5 million in the first year of a substantial coaching intervention underpinning significant organizational change. Initially, they concentrated upon the managing directors of the business units and their executive teams, a total of 70 or 80 managers. Then they broadened out the programme within the Post Office Network. Beyond this initial investment, each individual business unit had to decide how (and whether) to continue to fund its own coaching programme. The view was that a coaching environment could not be imposed but had to be bought into by the individual teams after a 'taste' of the process. It was not expected that every business would commit but that a significant cadre would sign up (which happened), and the performance of these over time would be such that those who had not committed would notice the difference and eventually be persuaded. This process was described as 'creating bushfires in the hope of starting a conflagration'.

Consignia could not afford to invest in coaching for all managers, as the average cost per head was around £7,000 (representing a total potential investment of £210 million!), so their strategy was to achieve high impact in selected areas in order to stimulate interest from the rest along with a desire to share in the business benefits. One early benefit was the development of consultation processes: the new-style managers changed and enhanced them to ensure the consultations fed directly into the decision-making process and were seen to influence decisions. This was a refreshing change from going around in bureaucratic circles as in the past.

How it worked

Each manager who participated in the programme received around 25 hours of coaching. The first phase, the diagnostic, consisted of four or five sessions of two to three hours each over a short period of time, followed by a second, dynamic, phase in which the sessions typically lasted for about one hour every six weeks or so and were mostly face to face although some could be by telephone. Then, finally, an exit route was planned, with a debrief.

The coaching styles and approaches were deliberately varied, using several different firms of consultants: some stressed business performance and strategy, some focused on the managers' soft skills and some involved behavioural psychologists. One of the tools used was a leadership behaviour profile, a flexible instrument that could be implemented on a one-to-one basis or using a 360-degree feedback model.

In the course of this, the managers learnt the rudiments of coaching for implementation in an informal way on the job, and the business started to move towards the challenge of providing all its own coaching inputs. Some of the initial consultants trained internal coaches – indeed three senior managers who were unable to obtain managing director positions went on to become professional coaching consultants in their own right.

Looking to the future

Consignia is an organization in the throes of massive change. Graham Cater has moved on, and is now Chairman of the Post Office Board for Wales. He expects to see greater transformation in the next three years than in his previous 35 years in the organization – he hopes and believes the management team will be ready, equipped with their new coaching skills.

Guardians, networks and sponsors

A sixth technique is sometimes distinguished within this cluster, the 'role of a guardian', the meaning of which is obscure and which even defies conversion to a verb ('guarding'?). The concept sometimes seems to be used specifically to remove lower-level activities from the definition of mentoring, suggesting the guardian is a low-level mentor or adviser. It can perhaps best be understood as a primitive form of mentoring, but it does not seem to justify separate classification.

Networking is also a fairly low-level technique: even as a planned process with a facilitator, it is about little more than keeping in touch with others who may prove useful in the future. This is not to denigrate the technique, as it may prove invaluable to managers, especially in expanding narrow horizons. It can help open up opportunities for benchmarking good practice, or perhaps for partnership in using an external training provider. It is also an essential technique for any ambitious manager, when it is about making and cultivating contacts with a view to career progression.

Sponsorship is about a senior manager 'adopting' more junior colleagues to help them, and to be seen to help them, with their careers. Sponsoring is usually non-financial, although some organizations allocate control of development budgets to sponsors. More importantly, it is about the sponsor taking an interest in the careers of the managers s/he sponsors, assisting and protecting them, and making provision for their advancement. It is so similar as to be almost indistinguishable from the form of shadowing or role modelling described in Case Study 16. It borrows from clandestine and largely discredited practices, like nepotism or Freemasonry, but in a meritocratic way. It is a particularly widespread practice in the USA but less common in Europe, at least in its most overt form. As a planned, organization-wide technique it can be invaluable for succession planning.

Taken together, these techniques are likely to appeal most to reflectors and perhaps theorists, but at least one of them is likely to benefit every manager at some stage of his/her career. They are only expensive when premium-priced consultants are bought in; otherwise, there are virtually no oncosts, and usually good time/benefit and cost/benefit ratios. One possible pitfall for organizations is that they can get carried away with successes in certain specific circumstances and generalize this into treating coaching or mentoring as a universal panacea: better to be pragmatic and use these techniques selectively.

Executive coaching

At the most senior level, some organizations like to use coaching as a kind of remedial service for directors or other senior executives who need help with something specific. In this circumstance, the service is probably a combination of coaching and mentoring; indeed the whole range of techniques within this cluster could be deployed using one coach. One problem with this is that it tends to be a highly confidential service, as some organizational cultures frown upon what they perceive as a confession of deficiency. Understandably, therefore, some managers are not keen to demonstrate weakness by accepting coaching in this environment.

Case Study 20 – Colin George

Colin George is an independent consultant with a portfolio of interests, which include chairmanship of the Lifelong Learning Foundation. He specializes in providing executive coaching, one to one, to senior managers of large organizations. As a former Group Personnel Director of

Guinness plc (prior to the merger that formed Diageo) and a past Managing Director of Guinness Enterprises, he has the ideal background to relate to the issues affecting his clients.

Most of his individual clients come from personal referrals, often on a confidential basis; all are directors or managers from the most senior levels of large organizations. His corporate client list includes companies such as Diageo, Barclays Bank, CGNU and major voluntary organizations like the National Trust for England and Wales.

Getting started

Colin is brought into a company either at the personal behest of the individual client (who may sometimes also be the HR director), or to meet the needs of a programme inspired by, or managed by, the HR function. The company may already have senior people with coaching and mentoring skills, such as the HR director (again) or a management development manager, but these people may not have the appropriate stature for the prospective individual client or the time to take on the assignment or it may just be that the company desires a fresh, external viewpoint.

At the most senior levels, Colin feels the distinctions between coaching and mentoring become blurred: his role may be to act as a sounding board, offering a questioning approach (ie coaching) or it may be to provide the direct benefit of his experience (mentoring) or more likely it may be a bit of both. It may be a stand-alone service, or an adjunct to more formal education in the form of courses and workshops. He finds himself usually more concerned with process than content – looking at how managers do things rather than what they do.

The coaching process

His service involves an initial meeting to see if the personal chemistry is right, to exchange information and to scope out the client's expectations. Thereafter, sessions normally take place face to face (or occasionally by phone) and last for about two hours each time. These will typically occur monthly, although in certain circumstances, where the need is more urgent, they have sometimes been as often as weekly.

At the end of each session, the two participants agree two or three areas to consider at the next session, and when that will be. It's an informal arrangement: the service is not rigidly objective-driven, but tends to be rather looser, almost taking the form of general counselling. The agenda is flexible: they look at areas like how to think more strategically, the client's relationship with his/her boss, getting the team to work more effectively or whatever is of most concern to the manager.

About a third of Colin George's clients are managers who are moving from a functional role into a predominantly managerial one – either in fact, or in their minds, having made the *de facto* move some time before – or are taking on substantially greater management responsibilities. One recent example was a group finance director who had become the chief executive, a logical and fairly common move but one that greatly expanded that individual's horizons. Another third of clients are HR directors, who are often among the first to see the need for this service. The remaining third are a disparate group who simply 'feel a need' for a sounding board or an alternative thinking style.

One client was a board-level director, an intelligent, able but often very flippant character, who liked to needle colleagues with shrewd but cutting observations. Naturally this made him rather unpopular with his peers, who tended to find subtle ways to get their own back. As a result the director's career was blocked, and he found himself unable to achieve the top job he aspired to. All of this became apparent during the coaching sessions, and the solution was obvious – to change the obstructive personal behaviour. Of course, it is much easier to identify such a problem than to act to do something about it.

Timescales and outcomes

Colin's interventions last, on average, for about a year: some go on much longer, but the sessions tend to become much less frequent, while in an extreme case one ended after just a couple of sessions. Sometimes there can be unexpected problems, or the client may not really want to change, or there are practical difficulties with individuals' priorities – it's one thing to agree to put sessions in the diary, but quite another to fit them into an executive's busy and constantly shifting schedule. One of the biggest obstacles to a successful intervention is the unpredictability of events – work with one client was effectively suspended by an unexpected acquisition development, when Granada launched its hostile bid for Forte.

However, usually the outcome is positive. The timetable is often clear cut from the outset; the programme runs its course, and ends when the problems are sorted out and original issues are resolved. This is rarely a revelation, but a gradual process that may be measured by client confidence and the individual being settled into his/her new role. Sometimes sessions peter out over a lengthy period of time, rather than just coming to an abrupt end.

Colin George may be contacted at colingeorge@msn.com.

Further reading

Clutterbuck, D (1998) *Learning Alliances*, IPD, London
Lewis, G (1996) *The Mentoring Manager*, Prentice-Hall, London
Parsloe, E and Wray, M (2000) *Coaching and Mentoring*, Kogan Page. London
Whitmore, Sir J (1996) *Coaching for Performance*, Nicholas Brealey, London

TEAM BUILDING

Group-work	✔
Individual	

Naturally, managers spend a great deal of time working in groups, so it makes sense to look at how these groups can work more effectively and, borrowing the sporting metaphor, how they can be built into successful teams. The given in this situation is that team working is better than group working, since it represents co-ordinated effort rather than the prospective chaos of people in a nominal work group perhaps pulling in different directions.

It is wrong to consider team working per se as a development technique, since it lacks any form or structure, or scope for influence, and as such is merely a context (albeit an important one) for discovery learning (see later in the chapter). However, managers can be allocated specific roles, particularly that of team leader, and be subject to all sorts of planned interventions that transform the activity into team building or, in a term that some prefer, team development.

Team building is a crucial technique for encouraging co-operation, sharing of information and mutual credit for work well done: it works against narrow egotism, self-seeking individualized competition, isolationism and similar unhealthy trends. It seeks to prove the saying that the whole is greater than the sum of the parts. This should give some pointers to when this technique should be deployed.

Pros and cons

One possible drawback is that it is often difficult to single out individual performance within a team, at least from the point of view of an observer from outside the team. In assessing the team leader, one may have to be satisfied with measuring the performance of the team as a whole. Of course, some would argue that that is the whole point of the technique.

Team building should certainly appeal to activists and pragmatists, perhaps less so to reflectors and theorists. It will probably appeal to games players, as in practice there is a strong correlation between the two techniques.

In cost terms, it shares the characteristic of most of the on-the-job techniques that the oncosts are either not easily attributable or they are non-existent. However, formal team-building events may be expensive, particularly when facilitated by external consultants. Case Study 21 shows how one organization – and industry – avoided this pitfall.

Case Study 21 – Railtrack

The privatization of the UK railways in 1996 led to the creation of Railtrack Group plc, one of the largest commercial estate owners in Europe, which owns and runs the UK's national railway infrastructure. Railtrack employs around 11,000 staff and operates 20,000 miles of track, 9,000 level crossings, 750 tunnels, 2,500 railway stations, 40,000 viaducts and bridges, and 40,000 property units.

Every minute counts

A key measurement for Railtrack, jointly set with the government regulator, is minutes' delay to trains. The number of minutes trains spend on the tracks is Railtrack's responsibility, and significant delays can lead to the imposition of financial penalties. As the cost of delays amounts to as much as £400 per minute for busy stretches of track, it is not difficult to see that extensive delays could be very expensive to the railway industry. Accordingly, Railtrack has put in place a Process for Performance Improvement (PfPI) to address this issue.

The 1996 privatization, apart from creating Railtrack, also created 25 train operating companies (TOCs), two freight operators and a number of contractor companies, such as First Engineering – 40 different plcs in all. Initially, if a problem developed on one of the lines, account executives representing Railtrack and the TOC would meet and negotiate where responsibility lay, perhaps over a problem as trivial as a gap in fencing. The actions required to resolve a problem could be prolonged, and the time taken to reach a resolution inevitably led to more minutes' delays to trains.

At the time of its creation, Railtrack had a relatively bureaucratic structure. The country was divided into zones, each of which had a production manager, for example in the Midland zone, responsible for all lines, to whom reported area production managers responsible for a section of line, for example from Birmingham New Street (one of the UK's 14 biggest stations) to Crewe (historically, the hub of the network). Using the line in this example would be two principal TOCs (Virgin Trains and Central Trains), freight operator EWS and other TOCs passing through. Reporting to the area production manager was an area contracts manager, who contracted all contract suppliers for construction, maintenance and so on. This structure tended to move so slowly that it often led to more minutes being lost.

Setting up new teams

From 1998, area delivery groups (ADGs) were formed at Railtrack's initiation, involving all key parties who had an interest in a particular stretch of line, including TOCs, freight operators and contractors. The idea was to forge teams working together with a common purpose to improve the PfPI as a group, by making decisions there and then that could be implemented within an agreed budget. There are now 27 ADGs across the country, each including around 8 to 10 rail industry managers, each of whom has the authority to make a decision and is involved with that particular route. They follow a regular, monthly process, including an ADG meeting where they aim to resolve speedily all issues affecting the PfPI.

To support this initiative, Railtrack offered a programme of off-the-job team-building training for all the companies' key managers involved in the ADGs, piloted in 1998 and rolled out from 1999. Once the group had received the team-building training, they were then offered the support of real-time training, which was provided by an experienced person who could act as a coach, mentor or adviser to the team. The real-time trainer worked one to one with each key ADG team member, particularly the area production managers, helping them decide how to prioritize items and managing the new process.

The team-building process

The real-time trainers also sat in on ADG meetings and gave feedback both to individual team members and to the group as a whole (during breaks). The emphasis was on encouraging openness, in contrast to the former 'us and them' attitude from managers from each different company, and on developing interpersonal skills among what are traditionally very process-oriented managers.

In one instance, an ADG team member discussed and found the means to solve a problem, and made a call from his mobile phone, during the ADG meeting. Within a few hours, a delay of 2,000 minutes per week, costing £120 per minute, was resolved. This example was on a relatively cheap stretch of rural track.

Alec McPhedran, Railtrack's Corporate Leadership and Development Manager, hails the ADG process as a resounding success and an excellent example of how an HRD function can support primary drivers in the operational part of an organization. He remains cautious about the danger of the ADGs slipping back into the old ways of working. As new managers become involved in the process or replace those who received the initial support, there is a need to ensure the development is ongoing and still effective. He has acquired and developed the resources to enable the team-building process to continue to be available to ADGs. The development process and the team-building principles that underpin it are still in place, but no further external intervention is planned at present. Internal facilitators are being developed to help ensure the process is ongoing. Given the success of the ADG concept in improving performance, the model is now being tested in wider rail issues including the continuous improvement of safety in the UK railways.

Further reading

Belbin, M (1996) *Team Roles at Work*, Butterworth-Heinemann, Oxford
Newstrom, J and Scannell, E (1997) *The Big Book of Team Building Games*, Pfeiffer Wiley, New York
Stuart, R (1998) *Team Development Games for Trainers*, Gower, Aldershot

ACTION LEARNING

Group-work	✔
Individual	✔

This is also known as action-based learning, and sometimes bracketed with self-managed learning.

Action learning is a group development approach whereby managers come together in 'action learning sets' to exchange experiences of real work problems, ask questions of one another and collaborate on solutions, usually but not necessarily with the help of a facilitator. Its underlying assumption is that direct exposure to problem-solving situations makes better managers.

As its name suggests, it is based on the principle of 'taking action', which is to say it is not enough just to analyse a problem and/or recommend solutions: the managers have also to act on their recommendations to complete the process. It is a form of internal consultancy, whereby managers from within an organization identify the problems they are going to address, think them through and then do something about them.

Action learning can be used, and often has been, in an off-the-job context, particularly within academic programmes. But its purest form is unsimulated in the real work situation, as championed recently by many Japanese firms, although it originated in the work of Reg Revans and others in Britain in the 1960s. It may be seen as the on-the-job counterpart of open learning (see Chapter 5), as it comes from a similar tradition and shares the values of being learner-centred and work-based. But whereas open learning puts the emphasis on self-study of learning materials with a theoretical bias, action learning focuses on practical implementation of ideas.

There are similarities between action learning and quality circles, in that in both techniques' work groups come together to solve problems. However, the focus in quality circles is not on learning or development.

Pros and cons

The results of an action learning programme can be dramatic: it is not unusual for a programme to aim to achieve substantial financial benefits for a business and then to achieve that aim. However, it is essentially reactive and pragmatic in approach, inward-looking and lacking in imaginative input save what the managers bring to the table themselves. If practised regularly, say repeated every year, it must inevitably yield to the law of diminishing returns. Therefore it is probably best implemented with an external facilitator and in combination with some coursework or other formal input. On the other hand, for those managers used to a diet of theory, whose experiences of development have mainly been traditional courses, it can be a breath of fresh air.

Action learning should appeal most to activists and pragmatists, and probably least to theorists, although reflectors may gain something from it.

It typically costs no more or less to implement than practical coursework, open learning or work-based projects. Once it has demonstrated successful outcomes, notably financial benefits, it should compare favourably with alternatives, making it an attractive option in any highly cost-sensitive environment.

Case Study 22 – Huntsman Corporation

Huntsman Corporation, with headquarters in Salt Lake City, Utah, is North America's largest privately owned chemical company, with annual revenues of $7 billion. It has around 14,000 employees in facilities in 43 countries around the world. Huntsman manufactures basic products in not just the chemical industries, but also plastic, automotive, construction, textiles, healthcare and packaging (including manufacture of the Big Mac container for McDonald's).

In 1999 it doubled to its present size by the acquisition of four businesses from Imperial Chemical Industries (ICI). One of these is the Aromatics business, based at the North Tees site near Middlesbrough in north-east England, employing around 400 people in the processing of petrochemical products. This had been an ailing business, suffering from under-investment under ICI ownership, which the new Huntsman management aimed to turn around.

Securing commitment

Huntsman entered into a compact with the workforce, requiring them to contribute to the rescue of the business – the company invested £35 million in a training and development programme on the condition that local management and employees committed their time and efforts to achieving change. Priority targets were an increase in plant output (the target was to double it at least) and an improvement in production reliability.

External facilitators were brought in to lead an action learning initiative for managers and employees alike. This programme began around mid-1999 and is scheduled to reach completion by early 2002, although this is more of a handover, as the external facilitators prepare to empower internal facilitators to pick up where they leave off. Thus action learning is planned to be ongoing.

Developing competence

The programme began with the identification of site-specific competences and measurement against them, building a picture of where the business was then and where it wanted to be two years thence. The corporate objectives were reaffirmed, and the training intervention began.

The core of the programme consisted of 'toolbox sessions', on-the-job learning with additional, complementary training input. These sessions were typically around three-quarters of an hour long with additional time for review, based at the workplace but supported by text-based training materials. The materials were bespoke, using some theory along with many practical examples from the plant, and ran to an average of 10–15 pages. They included pre-session work for the learner and instructional tools for the supporting manager.

The toolbox sessions were then reinforced by off-the-job workshops, but the bulk of the learning and corresponding action for change took place at the point of work. In fact, 87 per cent of learning was measured as taking place on the job, which with over 10,000 recorded learning hours represents a sizeable saving against the potential time lost away from work at training.

First-line managers

An important finding was that first-line managers had a key role to play in leading initiatives and supporting employees, and these managers are among those identified to take forward the internal facilitator roles, along with operations and technical managers.

Among the positive outcomes recorded so far are:

- significant cost savings (yet to be quantified);
- the identification of a range of training needs, some of which have begun to be addressed;
- the development of a learning culture in which everyone expects learning to be a continuous part of the job;
- the development of a more team-based approach to work and problem solving;
- the identification of a number of new key performance indicators for both people management aspects (eg attendance management) and operational management aspects (technical issues);
- output has indeed doubled, from around 500,000 tonnes to over 1 million tonnes.

Overall, the programme is judged to have been a great success, and has helped secure the future of the business.

Further reading

Pedler, M (ed) (1998) *Action Learning in Practice*, Gower, Aldershot
Revans, R (1998) *ABC of Action Learning*, Lemos and Crane, London

Web references

www.action-learning.org
www.free-press.com/journals/gabal/articles/gabal-article-002.htm
www.mcb.co.uk/imc/action-l.htm

WORK-BASED PROJECTS

Group-work	✔
Individual	✔

These are also known as work-based assignments or sometimes as special projects or, when carried out by groups, as task forces or working parties.

We have already examined projects as an off-the-job development technique; they are perhaps even more prevalent, and frequently much more extensive in scope, when carried out in a real work situation. They are sometimes emphasized as 'special projects', particularly when they are intended to be primarily developmental in nature. They may be individual or team-led. They are often ambitious in scope but need not be; for example, 'task forces' is one term for a simple project with a short-term focus, tackled by a team.

Unlike projects within courses, they are almost always real-life assignments as distinct from artificial simulations. They tend to be longer-term. And they need not result in a written report or presentation; often an informal report will suffice. Sometimes the project will lead seamlessly into another project or dissolve naturally into other work. In other words, they reflect some of the chaos of ordinary life and work.

Uses and applications

As previously noted, projects lend themselves to use for assessment purposes. The project has become a common device for generating evidence of competence for inclusion in a portfolio, such as in an NVQ programme.

A work-based project is usually an integrated programme of work with a predetermined goal or concept. It can run for any period of time from a few days to several years, it can involve budgets from zero to millions of pounds and it can be operational or strategic in scope. Typically, managers are given full responsibility for taking the decisions that affect them. Overall, the project provides a structured context for a manager to undertake development in a real work context under 'ring-fenced' conditions.

Some organizations go so far as to operate a project-based management strategy or policy, where managers are organized into project teams that are at least as important as their line responsibilities, where there is a permanent matrix management structure and where projects are a continuous way of life. At the other extreme, there may be organizations where managers never get the opportunity to lead or participate in project work. In either of these scenarios, and the more common positions in between, the project remains a legitimate means for facilitating management development.

Pros and cons

Projects share the characteristics of other self-managed learning techniques, like action learning and team building, of efficiently drawing upon integral learning resources but tending to underutilize external resources that could enhance the effectiveness of the learning. They can be invaluable in helping inculcate a learning culture and in broadening managers' understanding of how development occurs, provided they form part of a wider portfolio of management development methods within an organization.

Theorists will enjoy projects – the bigger the better – and project teams should provide ample scope to address the needs of activists, reflectors and pragmatists.

The costs of this technique depend on the scale and scope of what is being attempted – and any financial gains are likely to be in proportion. This makes it impossible to characterize projects as either expensive or cheap – it depends on the circumstances.

Case Study 23 – Bank of Scotland

Bank of Scotland dates back to 1695, when it was established by Act of the (then) Scottish Parliament, making it the oldest surviving UK clearing bank. It has 21,000 staff, 325 branches, mainly in Scotland, and corporate offices in England, France, Germany, Russia, USA and Hong Kong.

Among its extensive range of management development activities, the Bank runs a number of management development programmes for 'high-potential' managers. There are around 300 managers working on these at the moment, focusing on Bank-specific competences concerned with leadership behaviours. Some programmes, such as workshops, are mandatory, and some are voluntary, such as the use of selected materials from a learning resource centre, while managers have to be nominated for certain other programmes, including participation in cross-functional projects.

Cross-functional projects

The Bank's management development team operates a constant programme of cross-functional projects, which address broad corporate issues, and emphasize collaboration through networking and working around the organization. Managers are nominated by a steering group, which includes the chief executives of the Bank's main divisions (personal, business and corporate banking), group functions and human resources. The same steering group also identifies the topics to be addressed by projects, enabling the management development team to match the development needs of individual managers to the topics. The management development team then forms project teams of people from different business areas, and negotiates their release from their regular duties for one month, usually with a minimum of six weeks' notice.

The project team's remit is to make recommendations on the topic and do all the work needed to get to that stage. This means the issues have to be manageable and the goals achievable within a month, and the project has to be very practical. Occasionally, a project team member may be asked to go on to implement the project's recommendations, but more usually the process stops, for the participants, at the recommendation stage.

Recent project topics have included:

- investigating regional branding for deposit products;
- identifying opportunities for expatriate banking packages for international companies;
- knowledge management – what the bank should be doing;
- developing closer relationships with government committees and quangos;
- analysis of the international trade finance market;
- investigating new product potential arising from European Monetary Union.

The project process

At the outset, the project team comes together for a briefing by its sponsor – someone at managing director level or above – and scopes out the brief to specify the outcomes. A research phase follows, during which the team undertakes all the necessary work to reach its conclusions. Then there is the report, which will vary in length from 10 to 70 pages, and a presentation rehearsal with the management development team, who offer constructive feedback. Finally, the project team makes its formal presentation to a divisional board – or occasionally the group management board.

The learning opportunities inherent in the projects are around the task, which facilitates the acquisition of knowledge about both the Bank and external organizations, and around the process, particularly in terms of how the team forms. There are valuable lessons to be learnt about making contacts and handling internal politics.

For the management development team, the projects are very labour-intensive, as it has to organize facilities and expenses for each project team and ensure administrative support, but it is nevertheless considered a very worthwhile programme.

Julia Stevenson, the Bank's Director of Management Development, says:

> The benefits of this approach to both the business areas and the individuals are considerable. Many of our projects have improved the service we offer to our customers and have resulted in either reduced costs, or increased revenue for the Bank. Others have given us a useful insight into what our strategy should be when going forward. From the developmental point of view, our managers have enhanced their knowledge of the businesses in which they operate as well as their project management, report-writing and presentation skills. Hopefully they have also built a very useful set of contacts for the future.

Further reading

Bee, F and Bee, R (1997) *Project Management: The people challenge*, IPD, London
Smith, B and Dodds, B (1997) *Developing Managers Through Project-Based Learning*, Gower, Aldershot

Web reference

www.apm.org.uk

PERFORMANCE AND DEVELOPMENT REVIEW

Group-work	
Individual	✔

This is also known as appraisal or performance appraisal (although neither of these terms conveys the developmental aspect).

This is the process by which a manager interviews subordinate managers or other employees in order to review their performance and seek to improve it. Performance and development review may be seen as part of a wider process of performance improvement, embracing concepts like human performance technology and other systems.

Arguably, this technique should have been included under the section on off-the-job techniques, as the actual review takes place in a one-to-one interview that by necessity is off the job. It is included here because its focus is on the job: it dwells upon what has been happening in the workplace and what the participants want to happen in the near future. While the interview is off the job, the whole process involves managers in thinking about their work as they perform it, learning and improving on the job, before and after the interview. Often it is linked to the production and pursuit of a personal development plan (see later in the chapter).

In this way, this technique can be seen as an extension of the coaching cluster, or as one of its most formal forms, providing a forum to discuss the work situation and to seek to improve what the manager is doing. Increasingly, not just in management development, performance improvement is being seen as the whole point of learning: that is certainly the focus with this technique.

It is possible to operate an entire performance development and review system on a competence basis. Some organizations have competence-based job roles and job descriptions, which means they have to have competence-based performance management systems, which means development tends to be competence-based too.

The old term for this technique, 'appraisal', although still common, is less preferred because it accents the judgemental rather than the developmental. In some organizations, trade unions have long opposed 'appraisal' and all its connotations, and HR managers have had to find other terminology to support such initiatives.

360-degree feedback

This is also known as 360-degree appraisal or, occasionally, multi-source feedback, multi-rater assessment, upward feedback or peer evaluation.

Increasingly, performance review is seen not just as a one-to-one exchange between an employee/manager and his/her manager, but as a question for a broader audience within the organization (and occasionally beyond it). The review process is 360-degree feedback when it extends to include a manager's peers and subordinates, and perhaps other colleagues whose roles impinge on the subject's; and, in some cases, contacts from external organizations, notably customers, but also suppliers or other business partners.

The origins of the term are sometimes explained like this: 90-degree appraisal refers to a traditional, downward appraisal; 180-degree appraisal adds upward feedback; 270-degree appraisal includes the views of subordinates and peers; 360-degree adds all individual 'appraisees' and their superiors; and finally, 450-degree appraisal adds in customers and suppliers. The simpler explanation is that 360-degree feedback conveys a sense of consulting the full circle of concerned parties.

The technique of 360-degree feedback has been criticized for generating too much paperwork and therefore being a cumbersome and sometimes bureaucratic process. However, Web-enabled technology is easing these problems, both by reducing unnecessary paper and by speeding things up, especially with large numbers of participants spread over a wide area.

Pros and cons

When performance review becomes this more inclusive process, and more an open discussion than a dialogue, it opens up greater potential for organizational development. It also stands more chance of being successful, as it caters for a wider range of learning style preferences: whereas the traditional appraisal interview would have appeal probably only for reflectors, the broader process can inspire theorists and pragmatists too.

Formal performance development and review systems can be quite expensive to implement, but often these costs are associated with initial set-up and are not sustained. Equally often, they are to do with marketing the service, and winning hearts and minds within the organization, rather than the routine of implementation. It is possible to tailor the concept, design and marketing costs to fit any organization's budget, however large or small.

Case Study 24 – Scottish Power

In the 10 years since the UK government privatized the former South of Scotland Electricity Board, the organization has grown into a major international energy and utilities company, bolstered by a number of acquisitions, including ManWeb, Southern Water and PacifiCorp. Scottish Power plc now employs around 24,000 people and provides energy to millions of business and domestic customers in the UK and the western United States. Its utilities include electricity, gas and water services, plus Internet and telecommunications services provided through its majority-owned subsidiary, Thus.

In 1996, Scottish Power's energy supply division embarked upon a major performance management and improvement initiative for all managers and staff in the division, which includes most of the company's customer service and call centre operations, and a total of around 800 employees. Its aims were to raise individual and business performance levels, encourage learning and development, and stimulate a culture of continuous improvement.

Partnership and training

The initiative was developed in partnership with the trade unions, involving not merely negotiation or consultation but genuine partnership based on mutual trust, sharing of ideas and opinions, and a shared set of business values. This took longer than simply driving the process, at the insistence of senior management and the HR function, but was well worth it in terms of the benefit of having a system that works and to which everybody shares a commitment.

The new system was initiated by a programme of training. This took the form of two workshops, one for the managers who would be conducting the reviews and one for all managers and staff, all of whom would be on the receiving end. With between 8 and 12 participants in each workshop, taking place at the rate of one or two per week, this meant the workshop programme lasted for about a year. As a follow-up, each participant received a self-study workbook, commissioned specifically for Scottish Power. Further training workshops were organized around issues like coaching, mentoring, self-confidence and assertiveness. Altogether, this introductory training process lasted until 1998.

The review cycle

Once established, the system consisted of three phases:

- self-review;
- performance review and objective setting;
- development review.

In the self-review phase, the individual was asked to rate his/her current performance in the key areas of teamwork, customer focus, communication and business contribution. Managers under review had additionally to consider their leadership performance, including planning, organizing and monitoring work, developing and coaching staff, effective change management and 'living the values'. Individuals also had to consider their future, answering questions like 'Do you need further training?' and 'How would you like to see your career developing?' The completed self-review then became an input to the performance review meeting.

The next phase, performance review and objective setting, involved a meeting and the completion of a performance review form addressing the same areas as the self-review, followed by agreement of forward objectives. These had to be SMART objectives (specific, measurable, achievable, relevant and time-bound).

The third phase, development review, followed the agreement of objectives, and included the creation of a development plan for each employee, specifying job development and personal development to be undertaken in the period ahead. This was recorded on the development review form and became part of the process in the next cycle, subject to the same review.

Overall this system worked well, but it has evolved in practice to incorporate sensible changes. In 2001 it was extended to link directly to grading and pay awards, but the essentials of the system, including the strong developmental element, remain in place.

Case Study 25 – Philips

Amsterdam-based Koninklijke Philips Electronics NV is a global giant, with 200 production sites in over 25 countries, and sales and service outlets in 150 countries, employing over 200,000 people worldwide. The brand name of Philips is known in many markets, from lighting to consumer electronic goods, to semiconductors, to medical systems. Philips recognizes the vital significance of developing its managers to help sustain its competitiveness and to spearhead its drive to attain world-class excellence.

Career development

Among other initiatives, the company operates a career development programme, which embraces a range of activities such as work simulation exercises, psychometric assessments and coaching. A key component of the programme is 360-degree feedback, which is used exclusively for development and not assessment purposes, in order to encourage a frank and open climate.

Rather than use an off-the-shelf 360-degree feedback package, Philips have commissioned their own bespoke version, which is based on their in-company leadership competences. The documentation is easy and simple to complete, fits the corporate culture and utilizes information technology, with e-mail distribution and computer-scanned answer sheets.

The outputs include a personalized, confidential report for each participating manager, featuring ideas and activities to address his/her highlighted development needs. The managers also have access to a leadership development pack, which provides more general ideas and guidance.

This system ensures a clear, public development platform for managers to see for themselves how they compare to the world-class standard required and what they have to do to achieve career progression.

Further reading

Armstrong, M (2000) *Performance Management*, Kogan Page, London
Bahra, N (1997) *360-degree Appraisal*, FT Pitman, London
Hunt, N (1999) *Managing Performance Reviews*, How To Books, Oxford
Ward, P (1997) *360-degree Feedback*, IPD, London

Web references

www.ispi.org
www.the360.co.uk
www.360-degreefeedback.com

FORMS OF LEARNING RECORD

Group-work	
Individual	✔

In the same vein as the performance review, encouraging managers to record their learning progress serves as a useful means of both driving that learning to happen and reinforcing awareness of what has been learnt. (There is also a parallel with formative assessment.) It is an essential element of any competence development system, but its use is not restricted to that context.

This section looks at the four main types of learning records:

- learning logs and diaries;
- learning contracts;
- personal development plans;
- portfolios.

Learning logs and diaries

The traditional way of keeping a learning record is via a learning log or diary, in paper or (less traditional) electronic formats. Essentially, managers are required to make a precise written record of what they have learnt, often following a prescribed form – what has been learnt, how, who or what in particular helped, how long it took, etc.

This may be especially useful when managers are following a programme over a long period of time, so that they can refer back to earlier records as needed, or it may help support an intensive programme where a lot of theoretical content has to be covered and an additional record can act as a memory jogger. Unfortunately, managers may find it laborious to maintain these records and may object to the extra workload to the extent that either they complete the logs or diaries inadequately or they rebel against completing them at all. Reflectors will take to this technique naturally, while those who prefer other learning styles may wonder why they should bother.

Learning contracts

Sometimes trainers ask managers to agree learning contracts at the outset of some management development. Their rationale is that managers are implicitly agreeing to accept a certain set of responsibilities, and so it helps to make them explicit.

The learning contract is a document usually written in advance by the trainer, but sometimes drawn up in consultation with the manager when a programme begins. It is signed by both trainer and manager, and sometimes by others such as the manager's line manager, or perhaps another mentor, or other managers in the learning group. It records the development that it is agreed will take place, and who will do what to help make it happen.

For short development activities or events, this is probably over-egging the pudding, but as a technique to aid learning it can successfully complement long programmes such as courses, open learning (see Chapter 5), action learning (see earlier in the chapter), etc. It will appeal to theorists.

Personal development plans

Personal development plans are individual records that may be used to map out the direction a manager's development will take, and perhaps specify some inputs. Sometimes they are known as learning plans or simply action plans. There is a danger that they may become too prescriptive, with managers sticking to outdated or outmoded plans rather than thinking creatively. But many managers find it helpful to put down on paper – or in an electronic format – how they plan to pursue their development. Some programmes insist on incorporating a personal development plan to act as a signpost to development activities.

Portfolios

An increasingly common form of learning record is the portfolio, which is deployed in the UK National Vocational Qualification

(NVQ) system to demonstrate attainment of management competences, and may be put to a variety of other uses in management development.

The portfolio is a highly structured log, consisting of various pro forma documents with supporting 'evidence' drawn from the manager's work experience. The name comes from the notion that examples of the manager's written work are brought together into a file in the same way as with an artist or writer's portfolio. While the log or diary may occasionally be used for assessment purposes, this is almost always the main point of the portfolio. Again, learners often find them useful as learning devices in their own right.

The main criticism of the log applies even more so to the portfolio: it can be very laborious to put together a portfolio, to the extent that it tests the skills of a manager in selecting, writing, editing and compiling information. Depending upon the aims of the development, this can be an advantage or a disadvantage. A manager with a theoretical bent who gets involved in building a portfolio may become lost in the process at the expense of the content. Electronic versions may reduce the paper involved, but they don't reduce the volume of content.

Another criticism is that portfolios are often used in the spirit of APL, when the point is to record what has already been learnt or attained. Taken alone, this stands in contrast to a developmental purpose, looking backward rather than forward but, as with all techniques in this section, it can be useful to record what has happened, provided it is intended as an aid to what is going to happen.

Costs

Insofar as it can be time-consuming to fill out learning records, they can be quite costly, but these costs tend to be hidden, and there is usually a visible return. Producing records using in-house resources, from photocopying to desktop publishing, can be quite cheap, while professionally published versions may be glossy, sophisticated and very expensive.

Case Study 26 – The MCI NVQ portfolio

Since 1986, the UK government has recognized organizations representing every occupational area in the country as industry lead bodies, charged, among other things, with devising and maintaining national standards for their industries or occupational areas. In the area of management, that body is the MCI, which is part of the Forum for Management Education and Development. The initials formerly stood for Management Charter Initiative, after the notion that management should become a 'chartered' profession, like accountancy or engineering; since this notion has been abandoned, MCI has preferred to be known by the acronym.

MCI publishes a suite of National Management Standards, which can be configured into qualifications at three levels, equating to the UK National Vocational Qualifications (NVQs) at levels 3, 4 and 5. There are more specialized NVQs in project management, quality management and energy management, an NVQ in operations management at level 5, an NVQ in strategic management at level 5 and (generic) management NVQs at levels 3 and 4. (In Scotland, NVQs are known instead as SVQs or Scottish Vocational Qualifications – see Case Study 14 – but their format is identical and, while some occupational competences differ, the management standards are the same.)

Building the portfolio

The most common way to record and assess managers' attainments of these standards, or competences, is by using a portfolio of evidence (assessment of NVQs is either 'direct', for example by observation, at the lower levels, or by assessment of diverse evidence, as in the case of the management NVQs). MCI permits other forms of assessment, but they have to meet at least the requirements of the portfolio, and in any case the main other options are to present a verbal portfolio (with supporting written notes) or otherwise generate a virtual portfolio. Many leading management development providers and NVQ awarding bodies publish their own versions of these portfolios, but they all have consistent features.

The portfolio typically takes the form of a ring-binder containing a set of pro forma documents that help to map out the competences in relation to the NVQ candidate (the manager)'s job. This is incredibly detailed, as each standard or 'unit of competence' is broken down into 'elements of competence', and each of these elements is broken down into 'performance criteria'. Thus, at NVQ level 4, there are nine units of competence, comprising up to 31 elements of competence (depending upon which optional standards are chosen), in turn comprising 202 performance criteria. To attain this award, the manager has to record in his/her portfolio satisfactory evidence of competence for each of these 200 or so criteria.

The documentary contents of the portfolio ring-binder typically include: a full set of the standards in all their detail, forms to record personal and job information to help 'signpost' the finished work, an evidence indexing grid, further grids for evidence cross-referencing matrices, forms for translating the broad language of the standards to the specific language of the manager's job, whatever other forms the publisher considers necessary and advice notes on the use of all this material.

Gathering evidence

The process the manager will follow is to contextualize all this material into his/her own job, fill out the forms accordingly and compile written evidence into a folder (or, more usually, several folders), following the recommended structure. The completed portfolio should consist of a series of short narratives explaining how the manager meets each standard, backed up by a collection of written evidence, such as copies of letters, memos, minutes of meetings and testimonials from colleagues. The result should be a package of information proving to the assessor(s), acting for the awarding body, that the manager meets the standards at the appropriate level and is therefore entitled to an NVQ award.

For the manager's employer, this helps measure the manager's performance and that of his/her colleagues against national benchmarks, providing an index of the capabilities of the organization as a whole. It can provide a structure for managerial grading, progression, promotion and rewards. It should help motivate the manager through the award of the NVQ. It can also help with customer contract compliance and the attainment of organizational standards like Investors in People.

Further reading

Boak, G (1998) *A Complete Guide to Learning Contracts*, Gower, Aldershot

DISCOVERY LEARNING

Group-work	
Individual	✔

The last on-the-job technique is one of the simplest. Discovery learning happens all the time, but is rarely classified as a management development technique, as it is assumed always to be accidental – the kind of learning that happens in default of any planned training or development intervention. However, it is possible to plan for managers to learn things 'for themselves', by exposing them to situations where they are bound to discover problems and (it is hoped) solutions. Some people describe this as structured learning or a structured experience.

Discovery learning is the sort of thing Alan Mumford means when he refers to 'informal managerial – accidental processes' (see Chapter 2). As Mumford indicates, it is possible to move forward from this into 'integrated' or 'opportunistic' processes by planning for them to occur.

Meredith Belbin has been another notable champion of discovery learning as an explicit development technique, although his best-known deployment, as with most trainers, was with lower-grade staff, not managers. (Belbin pioneered the technique in the 1960s, to train railway employees in the principles of electricity.)

In the 1980s, the Open College offered an introductory course in learning skills in the form of an open learning workbook. The idea was that learners would 'discover' for themselves the advantages of open learning through experiencing the process. Learners who completed this workbook were subsequently offered open learning packs in management and other subjects.

This technique is one that will probably only occasionally be useful with managers because of the pitfall that it may seem patronizing. However, it is the natural learning process of both the activist and the pragmatist. An attraction for employers is that it is low in oncosts.

Becoming a trainer

Finally, there is an aspect of this that has already been mentioned but not in any detail: managers can develop themselves by taking responsibility for developing others. In discovery learning terms, the set assignment may be for the manager to act as a course tutor or lecturer, to lead an action learning programme, to be a coach, to review another's performance or to assume any of the other roles mentioned in the course of this book.

Who has not heard the old saw that one only really begins to understand a subject when one has to teach it? The same is true of being a trainer or developer, as in that role the manager discovers more particular knowledge, or accrues greater insight and understanding, than s/he ever obtained from being on the receiving end of these techniques. The manager discovers depths to the subject of which s/he was previously unaware.

Thus it may be helpful to a manager's development to expose him/her to this sort of opportunity, but care should be taken not to overextend managers, as failure in one of the more exposed roles could damage their confidence in carrying out their regular duties. Nevertheless, it is usually worth running the risk in the interests of stretching and challenging managers.

Case Study 27 – Kate Roberts

Kate Roberts is a retail management consultant, who works from an office base in her home in Berkshire, south-east England, with corporate clients in the Greater London area.

Her career in retail began in the early 1980s, when she took a part-time job as a checkout operator at her local supermarket while studying for a BSc degree at university. On graduating, she was offered a store management traineeship, and undertook a variety of roles in food retailing in several different stores UK-wide before settling into a customer service management position in a large London supermarket.

Managing customer service

This job involved a lot of day-to-day customer contact, as well as overall responsibility for meeting targets based on satisfying customer enquiries and reducing customer complaints. Kate found her manager rather process-driven, focused on statistics rather than people, and resistant to initiatives she suggested for changes in the way checkout and counter staff handled customers. However, she found an ally in the corporate headquarters' human resource department, and was able to argue successfully for implementation of a workshop-based staff training programme. What she didn't expect was to be told to deliver the programme herself.

Kate discovered that her training had prepared her to handle customer service issues herself to meet the requirements of her job, but not really to pass ideas on to other staff – at least not in a consistent way that would stand up to management scrutiny and to employees' annoying habit of asking obvious questions (to which the answers were maddeningly not so obvious).

A deeper understanding

After a false start with a not-too-successful workshop, Kate discovered – the hard way – that she needed to study her subject in more depth. She postponed the remaining series of workshops until she felt she had mastered the subject sufficiently, and obtained some learning resources from the HR department. Her second attempt was much more successful, with issues raised at the workshop that had not previously occurred to her: these were then built into subsequent workshops.

In the end, the workshops were so well received and so effective in her store that the HR department asked her to repeat the exercise for another store and then to train other customer service managers from around the country to implement the programme in their stores. The next stage was for Kate to be attached to the HR department to explore other programmes to be tested in one or two large stores before being rolled out nationwide.

Career progress

Kate went on to train for the Institute of Personnel and Development's Certificate in Training Practice, gained broader experience of the training and development function and later moved on to become a personnel and training manager with a non-food high-street retail chain. This served as a good foundation for the consulting career she now pursues: after a break to have children, she found it easier to work from home and establish her own consultancy practice. The learning potential of managers having to pass their knowledge and skills on to others is a valuable lesson she has never forgotten.

7

Looking forward

TAKING STOCK

There are a few conclusions we can draw from this survey of management development techniques.

First, there are a great many techniques available and plenty of opportunity for trainers to offer variety in their design of learning events. There should be a choice of techniques to suit every situation and every manager. There is no excuse for managers to find learning boring – in form as well as content – and, if they do, the trainer bears the burden of responsibility.

Note that there are plenty of both on-the-job and off-the-job techniques, and plenty of techniques both for individual development and for group development. Figure 7.1 presents them in a simple matrix.

Second, every organization needs to deploy a battery of techniques: none can get away with just using a few old favourites. The techniques represent a toolkit for developing not just managers but the organization, and they are the best means to ensure that talent is developed, careers provided for and succession planned.

Third, there are no wrong techniques – just wrong ways of using them. There is a time and a place for everything, and a technique to suit every learning style preference – it is up to the trainer to select

	Group-work	**Individual**
Off-the-job	courses games videos outdoor development open, flexible and distance learning e-learning development centres	courses external events and visits games videos psychometrics open, flexible and distance learning e-learning resource-based learning assessment techniques
On-the-job	team building action learning work-based projects forms of learning record discovery learning	sitting by Nellie instruction secondment coaching etc work-based projects performance and development review

Figure 7.1 Matrix of individual, group-work, off-the-job and on-the-job techniques

the most appropriate technique for the people and circumstances. Learners can also benefit from exploring how best they learn, recognizing their preferred style and perhaps identifying some favourite techniques, or, contrarily, by experimenting with techniques that are markedly different from their preferences.

Fourth, management development can benefit from exposure to new ideas drawn from different walks of life. Some of the most exciting techniques in this book are those that seemed most radical when first introduced and those for which the relevance to business management was initially questioned. This should lead us to a more open approach in the future and a greater willingness to accept and incorporate innovative methods. This not only expands our repertoire but also promotes creativity – both in ourselves and in others – which can only be to the gain of effective learning.

THE FUTURE OF MANAGEMENT DEVELOPMENT

Management development, like all learning, cannot stand still. Change – improvement and innovation – is taking place all the time, and this also applies to management development techniques. New techniques will emerge, and some will become popular, while some of the techniques in this book may soon be considered redundant for reasons not yet apparent to us. It is quite possible that, as you read this book, you will be aware of a new technique not known to the author at the time of writing.

However, it is instructive to look at the changes that have taken place over the past two decades or so. If we look back, we find that very few new techniques have emerged, and those that have are as a consequence of technological innovation. Had this book been written 10 years ago, it would not have included online learning or virtual learning centres, because the technology to support them did not exist. Arguably, it is not the techniques that have changed, merely the media: as we have observed, some say e-learning is just distance learning using new technology.

Where significant change has taken place, it is in the way techniques are used or in our understanding of how they work. It seems reasonable to predict that this trend will continue, and in the near future we will know more about how best to develop managers so that they learn more – and more efficiently – and perform better. Essential to this advance in our knowledge is a grasp of where we are and what we know now. If this book makes a small contribution to that, then I hope it has been worthwhile.

A–Z of management development techniques

Accelerated learning
Action learning
Action maze
Assessment techniques
Audio/video recording
Becoming a trainer
Benchmarking visits
Brainstorming
Buberian dialogue
Case history
Case studies
Closure
Coaching
Computer-based training
Conferences
Corporate universities
Correspondence courses
Counselling
Courses

Creative dialogue
Critical incident analysis
Demonstration
Deputizing
Development centres
Directed conversation
Discovery learning
Distance learning
Drama
E-learning
Encounter groups
Exchanges
Executive coaching
Exhibitions
Fish bowl exercise
Flexible learning
Games
Guided reading
Instruction

In-tray exercise
Job rotation
Jurisprudential framework
Lateral thinking
Learning contracts
Learning logs and diaries
Learning portals
Learning records
Learning resource centres
Lectures
Mentoring
Mind mapping
Networking
Non-verbal exercise
Online learning
Open learning
Outdoor development
Panel discussion
Performance and development
   review
Personal development plans
Portfolios
Problem pack
Programmed learning
Projects

Psychometrics
Question time
Resource-based learning
Role-play
Role-reversal
Secondment
Seminars
Shadowing
Sitting by Nellie
Small tutorial groups
Sponsoring
Storytelling
Structured debate
Syndicates
T-groups
Team building
Team teaching
360-degree feedback
Videos
Virtual learning centres
Virtual universities
Web-based learning
Work-based projects
Workshops

APPENDIX 2

Techniques and learning styles matrix

This matrix attempts to show the fit between management development techniques and preferred learning styles, and summarizes the points made in each section throughout the book. Not every technique discussed in the book is included in the matrix, as this would be unwieldy (there are over 80 techniques discussed, including the various coursework techniques), but the matrix should give an at-a-glance guide to the best fit between the main techniques and the four styles.

Please note that the fit between techniques and preferences is very much a matter of subjective judgement, in this case the author's, and different opinions may be equally valid. This model should be treated as a guide, rather than a definitive statement of fact.

Table A2.1 Techniques and learning styles matrix

	Activist	Reflector	Theorist	Pragmatist
Didactic Coursework	✘	~	~	~
Participative Coursework	✔	~	~	~
Conferences	✘	✔	✔	
Exhibitions	~	~		✔
Games	✔			
Videos	✘	✔	✔	
Psychometrics	✘	✔	✔	~
Outdoor Development	✔			~
Open/Distance Learning	✔	✔	✔	✔
E-learning	✔	✔	✔	✔
Resource-Based Learning		✔	✔	
Assessment Techniques	~	✔		✔
Development Centres	✔	✔	✔	✔
Sitting by Nellie	✔	~	✘	~
Instruction	✔			~
Secondment	✔	~	~	~
Coaching		✔	✔	~
Team Building	✔	✘	✘	✔
Action Learning	✔		✘	✔
Work-Based Projects	~	~	✔	~
Performance Review		✔	~	✔
Learning Records		✔		
Discovery Learning	✔			✔

✔ indicates a good fit

✘ indicates a poor fit

~ indicates a possible good fit
no mark indicates neutrality

Activists tend to prefer participative coursework, games, outdoor development, activity-based flexible learning, practical exercises in development centres, on-the-job activities like sitting by Nellie, instruction/demonstration (with practice) and discovery learning, secondments, team building and action learning.

Reflectors tend to prefer attending conferences, watching videos, using psychometric instruments, studying the content of open/distance learning and e-learning programmes, resource-based learning, formal assessments (including those that take place in development centres), coaching, performance and development review, and the use of learning records.

Theorists tend to prefer lectures, conferences, videos, psychometric instruments, the content of open/distance learning and e-learning programmes, resource-based learning, the broader, conceptual aspects of development centres and work-based projects, and coaching, at least at a theoretical level.

Pragmatists tend to prefer exhibitions, activities offered in distance learning and e-learning programmes (that can be tested at the workplace), some assessments and related aspects of development centres, team building, action learning, performance and development reviews, and discovery learning.

Index

16PF   69
360-degree feedback   37, 71, 129,
      148, 151–52

accelerated learning   44
accreditation of prior learning
      (APL)   33, 155
action-centred leadership   5
action learning   18, 19, 35, 38, 79,
      86, 112, 139–42, 144, 154, 160,
      164, 170–71
action maze   44
activist   *see* learning styles
Adair, John   5
American Management
      Association   26
American Society for Training and
      Development   59–60
Andromeda Training   62
appraisal   101, 147–49
Ashridge   100–02
   Directions (Ashridge journal)
      101
assessment   33, 34, 38, 43,
      56, 86, 91, 103–06, 143,

147, 155, 156–57, 164,
      170–71
   formative/summative assess-
      ment   103, 153
   self-assessment   70
assessment centres   107–08
asynchronous learning   77, 90
attachment   *see* secondment
audio recording   45
audio-visual aids   40, 54, 57

Baker Hughes   70–72
Balanced Scorecard   5
Bandler, Richard   5
Bank of Scotland   144–46
Barclay's Bank   132
Bass Brewers   33–34
becoming a trainer   160–62
Belbin, Meredith   69, 138, 159
benchmarking   57, 58, 130, 157
Blackboard   77, 91, 94
Body Shop, The   7
Boots   98
Boyatzkis, Richard   69
brainstorming   45

Brathay Hall Trust   73, 76
breakout group   *see* syndicate
British Airways   98
British Telecommunications (BT)
    63–65
Buber, Martin   45
Buberian dialogue   45
Business Excellence Model   5
Buzan, Tony   49
buzz group   *see* syndicate

Cadbury Schweppes   98
career development   3, 10, 25–26,
    30, 59, 151–52
case history   45–46
case studies   34, 40, 42–43, 45–46,
    105
CD ROM   88, 89, 93, 96, 97, 99,
    101
Central Trains   137
Certificate in Management (CM)
    33, 83
certification   33–34, 35, 37–38, 41,
    82–84, 103–06, 161
CGNU   132
chambers of commerce   121
charities   17, 100, 121, 122
Chartered Institute of Personnel
    and Development (CIPD)
    23, 30, 54, 59, 60, 72, 110, 134,
    146, 152
Citizens Financial Group   123
City University of Hong Kong   93
closure   46
coaching   17, 39, 64–65, 112, 113,
    122, 126–34, 137, 147, 150, 151,
    160, 164, 170–71
commando course   73
competence   9, 12, 26–27, 30, 38,
    43, 70, 74, 76, 80, 82–83, 86, 97,
    98, 99, 100, 101, 104, 106, 109,
    110, 111, 117, 124, 127, 141,
    143, 145, 147–48, 151, 153, 155,
    156–57

behavioural *versus* functional
    competence   27
    versus competency   26
    versus excellence   26
computer-based training   78, 88,
    96, 99
conference   16, 57–60, 170–71
    online conference   60
Consignia   127–30
Continuous Professional
    Development (CPD)   25
Coronation Street   53
Corporate Compendium, the
    63–65
corporate university   2, 81, 91
correspondence course   77, 90
counselling   17, 70, 107, 115,
    126–27, 133
courses   4, 8–9, 16, 18, 19, 31–54,
    55, 57, 61–62, 66, 69, 73, 74, 75,
    77, 78, 79, 80, 82, 86, 90, 92, 93,
    95, 97, 98, 100, 103, 105, 107,
    108, 117, 127, 132, 140, 143,
    154, 159, 160, 164, 169–71
Coverdale, Ralph   5
Coverdale training   5
creative dialogue   46
creativity   44, 45, 46, 49, 53–54, 58,
    61, 63, 118, 119, 154, 164
critical incident analysis   46

Dali, Salvador   54
de Bono, Edward   49
degree   12, 32, 160
demonstration   15, 105, 112,
    117–18, 171
Department for International
    Development (DFID)   35–37
deputizing   114
Deutsche Bank   101–02
development centres   26, 56, 69,
    107–10, 164, 170–71
Development Training Users Trust
    74

developmental assessment centres
   see development centres
Diageo   132
Diploma in Management Studies
   (DMS)   33–34, 83–84
Direct Line   123
directed conversation   47
discovery learning   15, 19, 59, 112,
   114, 126, 135, 159–62, 164,
   170–71
distance learning   39, 55, 77–84,
   87, 88, 89, 90, 97, 164, 165,
   170–71
District Audit   101
Docent   77, 91, 94
drama   47
DVD   66, 89

e-learning   56, 79, 88–94, 96,
   97–98, 101, 164, 165, 170–71
emotional intelligence   5, 42
encounter group   47–48
Ernst and Young   93
European Commission/Union
   125, 128
EWS   137
exchange   57, 58–59, 121, 122
executive coaching   131–34
exhibition   57–60, 170–71
experiential learning   16, 19–20,
   23
external events   55, 57–60, 164
extranet   77, 89, 149

Financial Times Group   93
First Engineering   136
fish bowl exercise   48
flexible learning   39, 41, 55, 77–87,
   97, 164, 171
Foreign and Commonwealth
   Office   35, 100
Forte   133
Forum for Management Education
   and Development   156

FT Dynamo   93

games   46, 49, 55, 61–65, 70, 136,
   138, 164, 170–71
George, Colin   131–34
Goleman, Daniel   69
graduate development   25,
   121–22
Granada   133
guardian   130
guided reading   95–96
Guinness   132
Gunning, Bob   123–25

haiku   53
Higher National Certificate (HNC)
   105
Honey, Peter   19, 20–21, 23
horse whispering   118
Huczynski, Andrej   67
human resource development
   (HRD)   16, 28, 138
human resource management   1,
   3, 34, 69, 119, 145, 161
Huntsman Corporation   140–42

ICI   140
illuminative incident analysis   47
Institute of Management   30, 102
Institute of Personnel and
   Development (IPD)   *see*
   Chartered Institute of
   Personnel and Development
instruction   7, 15, 111–12, 117–20,
   127, 164, 170–71
Intellinex   93
Interbrew   33
International Correspondence
   School   77
Internet   89, 101, 149
intranet   77, 89, 101
in-tray exercise   48
Investors in People (IIP)   5, 35, 64,
   157

job rotation 121–22
job swap *see* secondment
jurisprudential framework 49

knowledge management 2, 5, 93, 101, 114, 145
Kolb, David 20–21, 23, 69
Kolb's learning cycle 20
Kotler, Philip 2

laboratory training 41
lateral thinking 49
learner-centred learning 10, 16–17, 18, 19, 22, 139
learning contract 19, 34, 84, 153, 154, 158
learning diary 153
learning log 153
learning organization 2, 81, 85, 91, 97, 115
learning platforms 91
learning portal 91
learning records 112, 153–58, 164, 170–71
learning resource centre 93, 95, 96–102, 145
learning styles 4, 16, 20–23, 29, 41, 44, 69, 81, 84, 90, 107, 122, 149, 153, 163–64, 169–71
    activist 21, 40, 43, 44, 58, 63, 67, 70, 74, 97, 104, 118, 122, 136, 140, 144, 159, 170–71
    pragmatist 21, 44, 51, 58, 63, 70, 97, 104, 136, 140, 144, 149, 159, 170–71
    reflector 21, 43, 44, 58, 67, 70, 74, 92, 97, 104, 131, 136, 140, 144, 149, 153, 170–71
    theorist 21, 43, 44, 58, 67, 70, 92, 97, 114, 131, 136, 140, 144, 149, 154, 170–71
lecture 34, 37, 39, 40, 41, 50, 57, 67, 171
left/right brain 53

lifelong learning 2, 85
Lifelong Learning Foundation 131
Lotus Domino 101
Lotus Learning Space 77, 91, 94

Magritte, René 54
management standards 27, 156
Manchester Business School 118
Manpower Services Commission 8
ManWeb 149
Marks and Spencer 98
Martini 79
Master's degree in Business Administration (MBA) 32, 33–34, 84, 93, 100
McBer and Company 70
McDonald's 81, 140
McGraw-Hill Lifetime Learning 93
MCI 156–57
McKinsey 123–24
mentoring 39, 84, 113, 115, 126–27, 130, 131, 132, 134, 150
Michelin 62
Microsoft 40
mind mapping 49
m-learning 88–89
monodrama *see* drama
Motorola University 85–86
multi-rater feedback / assessment *see* 360-degree feedback
Mumford, Alan 16–18, 20–21, 23, 159
music 62
Myers-Briggs Type Indicator 69–72

Naidoo, Krib 118–20
National Commercial Bank of Scotland 123
National Extension College, the 78, 87

National Training Award   76
National Trust for England and
   Wales   132
National Vocational Qualifications
   (NVQs)   27, 143, 154–55,
   156–57
National Westminster Bank   123,
   124
Network Ireland   115–16
networking   17, 59, 60, 82, 126,
   130, 145
neuro-linguistic programming
   (NLP)   5, 86
non-verbal exercise   49-50
Nottingham Business School   33

Occupational Personality
   Questionnaire (OPQ)   69, 109
off-the-job   4, 8–9, 12, 18, 28, 29,
   44, 79, 55–110, 111, 115, 118,
   126, 127, 137, 139, 141, 143,
   147, 163
Oki   75–76
on-the-job   4, 9, 12, 18, 28, 29, 38,
   44, 59, 79, 102, 111–62, 163, 171
online learning   88–94, 97–98, 103,
   165; *see also* e-learning
Open Access Development Centre
   98–100
Open College, the   78, 159
open learning   19, 35, 38, 58, 74,
   77–87, 96, 103, 139, 140, 154,
   159, 164, 170–71
Open Tech programme   78
Open University, the   78, 80
organizational development   5, 7,
   12, 42, 115, 149
Otis   108–09
outdoor development   55, 73–76,
   164, 170–71
Outward Bound   73, 76
Overseas Development
   Administration   35
PacifiCorp   149

panel discussion   50
Parcelforce   127
performance and development
   review   26, 147–52, 164,
   170–71
personal development plan   76,
   101, 147, 153, 154
Philips   151-52
portfolio   34, 43, 104, 143, 154–57
Post Office   127
pragmatist   *see* learning styles
problem pack   48
programmed learning   78, 117
project   18, 34, 40, 42, 43–44, 83,
   105, 112, 123–24, 140, 143–46
Project Columbus   123–24
psychodrama   *see* drama
psychometrics   55, 69–72, 107,
   109, 164, 170–71

quality circles   139
question time   50
QuestionMark   91, 106

Railtrack   136–38
Redfern, Michael   52–54
reflector   *see* learning styles
resource-based learning   56, 88,
   95–102, 164, 170–71
Revans, Reg   139, 142
Roberts, Kate   160–62
Roddick, Anita   7
Rogerian group   *see* encounter
   group
Rogers, Carl   48
role play   50–51
role reversal   50–51
Royal Bank of Scotland   123–25
Royal Mail   127

samba drumming   53, 118
Saville and Holdsworth   69
Schulz, Will   48
Scottish Knowledge   93

Scottish Power   58, 102, 149–51
Scottish Qualifications Authority
    104–06
Scottish Vocational Education
    Council   104
Scottish Vocational Qualifications
    (SVQs)   105, 156
secondment   37, 59, 112, 121–25,
    164, 170–71
self-managed learning   18–19, 23,
    28, 139, 144
seminar   39, 40–41, 57
sensitivity training   41
shadowing   113–16, 130–31
simulation   45, 48, 65, 143, 151
    business simulation   62, 63, 65
sitting by Nellie   15, 19, 111–12,
    113–16, 164, 170–71
small tutorial group   39, 41
SMART objectives   150
sociodrama   *see* drama
Southern Water   149
sponsoring   33, 83, 113, 126,
    130–31, 146
Standard & Poor's   98
Standard Chartered Bank   81–84
Standard Life   98–100
Stirling Council   52
story telling   51
structured debate   51
succession planning   3, 25, 26, 76,
    107, 131
surrealism   54
synchronous learning   90
syndicates   34, 40, 42, 57

team building   46, 112, 135–38,
    144, 164, 170–71

team teaching   51–52
Terra Nova Training   75–76
Tesco   98
T-groups   41–42
theorist   *see* learning styles
Thus   149
Training Concepts   65
transfer   *see* secondment

Ulster Bank   123
United Technologies Corporation
    108

video   53, 55, 66–68, 70, 89, 97, 99,
    164, 170–71
    video conferencing   77, 88
    video recording   37, 45
Video Arts   66, 67–68
vignette   42
Virgin Trains   137
virtual learning centre   98, 100–02
virtual reality   88
virtual university   92
Volkswagen   100

Web-based learning   81, 90–91
Wireless Application Protocol
    (WAP)   88
W M Mercer   100
work-based project   18, 43, 112,
    140, 143–46, 164, 170–71
workshops   32, 39, 41, 52, 57, 59,
    82, 83, 84, 132, 141, 145, 150,
    161
'World Class'   64, 123, 151–52
World War II   67, 69, 73

Xerox Europe   100

Printed in the United Kingdom
by Lightning Source UK Ltd.
118711UK00001B/271-276

9 780749 436201